Jerry Snyder's

# Children's
## Songs for Guitar

### 100 songs for early childhood

## about the author

Jerry Snyder combines his knowledge of the guitar with a background as a music educator, author, clinician and professional musician. He is the author of a variety of guitar publications. His BASIC INSTRUCTOR GUITAR, which includes a Teacher's Edition, has been widely adopted by schools across the nation.

Other books that are arranged in a similar style to this folio include: BASIC SING BOOK FOR GUITAR, Hansen Catalog No. O299, SECOND BASIC SING BOOK FOR GUITAR, Hansen Catalog No. O421 and the BIG GOLDEN ENCYCLOPEDIA FOR GUITAR, Hansen Catalog No. R025.

## about the artist

Arthur Boos has an uncanny ability to capture the atmosphere of another time and another place with a fine, sure hand and to delineate character in a believable way. A talent in pen-and-ink drawing, such as that possessed by this artist, has not been seen for a generation.

His emphasis is on people. He portrays them with a rare compassion and understanding, be they pitiful waifs huddling in a doorway, joyful children or dejected and downhearted types.

The value of drawings to a book of this kind is immeasuable. They are presented here to delight the eye and for the enjoyment of children of all ages.

7414                                                        *The Publisher*

# alphabetical index

7414

# Key and rating index

7414

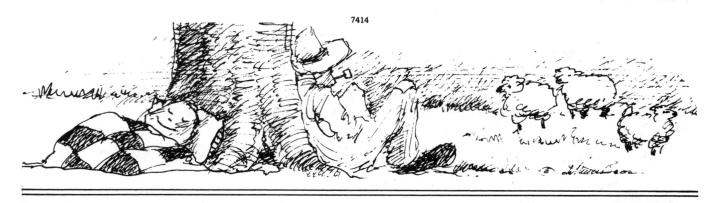

# Key and rating index

7414

# STRUMASONG

## in tablature GUIDE

1st string — E
2nd string — B
3rd string — G
4th string — D
5th string — A
6th string — E

**T A B**

**GLOSSARY**
Treble strings: 1st, 2nd and 3rd strings.
Bass strings: 4th, 5th and 6th strings.
Arpeggio: a broken-chord pattern.
root (R): the primary bass note in the chord; the bass note that gives the chord its name.
Fifth (5): the alternate bass note in the chord that is the fifth of the chord.
Accent ( > ): give emphasis or stress.

TABLATURE represents the six strings of the guitar.

The strum and finger patterns presented in this guide may be immediately applied to the C, B7, A7, A, Am or any five string chord. The patterns may be adapted to fit all other chord forms.

| SYMBOL | DESCRIPTION | SYMBOL | DESCRIPTION |
|---|---|---|---|
| | **BRUSH** — index and middle fingers strum down across the strings (bass to treble); strum at a 90 degree angle to the strings. | | **THUMB** — the thumb plucks the 5th string by pushing in toward the 4th string; keep the thumb straight and rigid. |
| | **SWEEP** — thumb strums downward across the string: (bass to treble); thumb sweeps perpendicular to the strings. | | **3rd FINGER** — the ring finger plucks the 1st string (E); primary movement comes from the knuckle. |
| | **SCRATCH** — index finger strums down across the strings (bass to treble); in this example only the 4th, 3rd, 2nd and 1st strings are strummed. | | **2nd FINGER** — the middle finger plucks the 2nd string (B); primary movement comes from the knuckle. |
| | **SCRATCH** — fleshy part of the index finger strums upward across the treble strings. | | **PLUCK** — ring, middle and index fingers pluck the treble strings (3rd, 2nd and 1st) together — simultaneously. |
| | **MUTE** — scratch down across the strings (bass to treble) and immediately mute or dampen (silence, deaden) the strings by rolling on to the side of the hand. | | **PINCH** — thumb and ring finger pinch or squeeze the strings together; keep the thumb rigid. |

# BRUSH

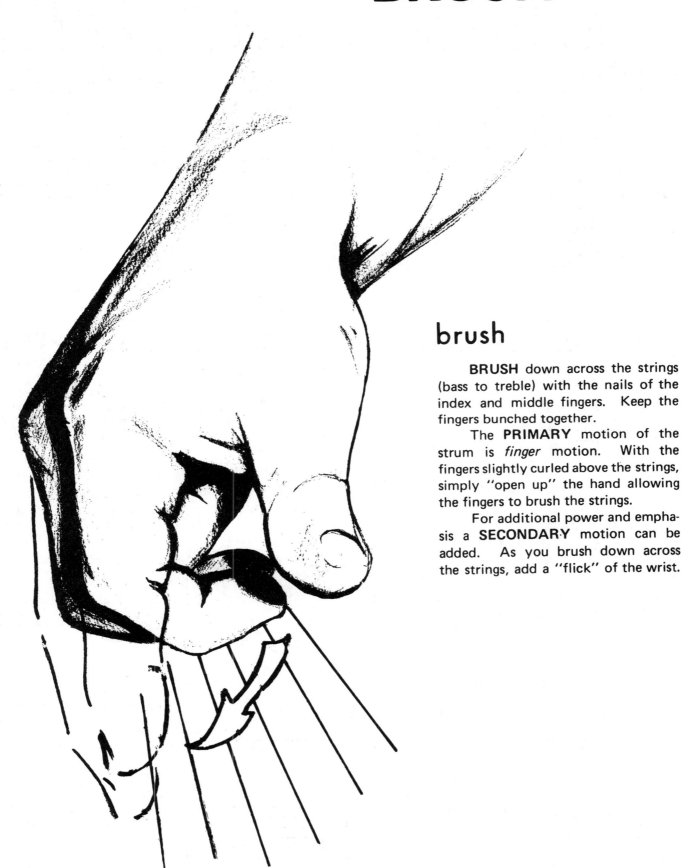

## brush

**BRUSH** down across the strings (bass to treble) with the nails of the index and middle fingers. Keep the fingers bunched together.

The **PRIMARY** motion of the strum is *finger* motion. With the fingers slightly curled above the strings, simply "open up" the hand allowing the fingers to brush the strings.

For additional power and emphasis a **SECONDARY** motion can be added. As you brush down across the strings, add a "flick" of the wrist.

# SWEEP

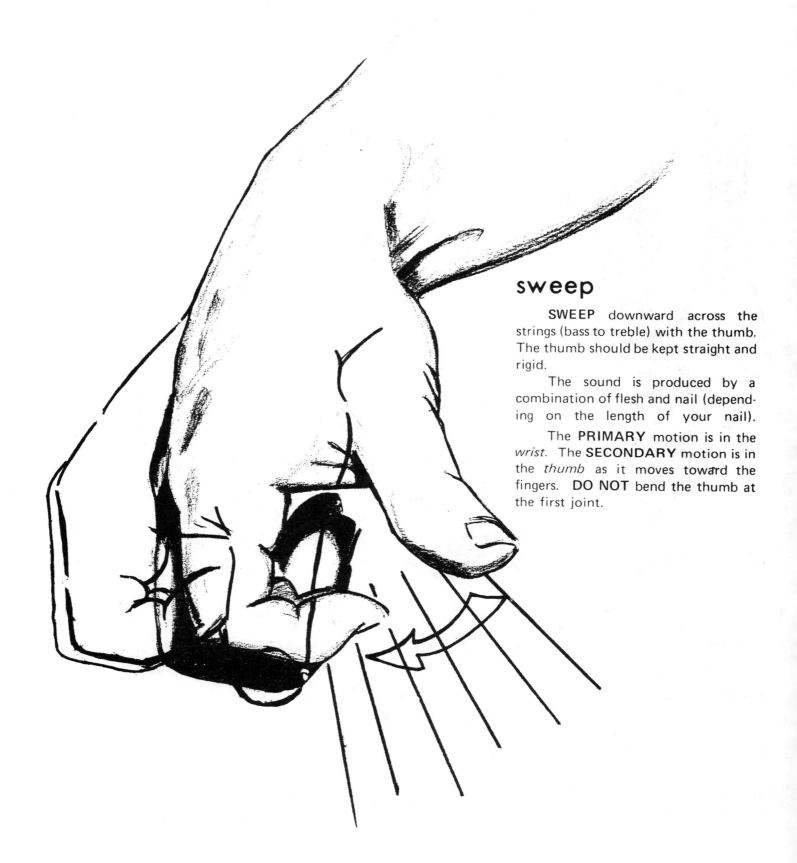

## sweep

SWEEP downward across the strings (bass to treble) with the thumb. The thumb should be kept straight and rigid.

The sound is produced by a combination of flesh and nail (depending on the length of your nail).

The **PRIMARY** motion is in the *wrist*. The **SECONDARY** motion is in the *thumb* as it moves toward the fingers. **DO NOT** bend the thumb at the first joint.

# SCRATCH

## scratch—down

SCRATCH down across the strings (bass to treble) with the nail of the index finger.

The **PRIMARY** motion of the strum is *finger* motion. Attempt to keep the hand above the strings.

*For additional* emphasis and power, add some *wrist* motion to the scratch. As you scratch downward, give a slight "flick" of the wrist.

## scratch—up

SCRATCH upward across the treble strings with the fleshy part of the index finger. It is only necessary to strum the 1st and 2nd strings.

The upward scratch is most often performed in alternation with the downward scratch; that is, scratch down-up-down-up, etc.

The **PRIMARY** motion of the strum is a *finger* motion with just a slight inward turning of the wrist.

When performing the scratch, keep the hand above the strings and use a *minimum* of motion.

# MUTE

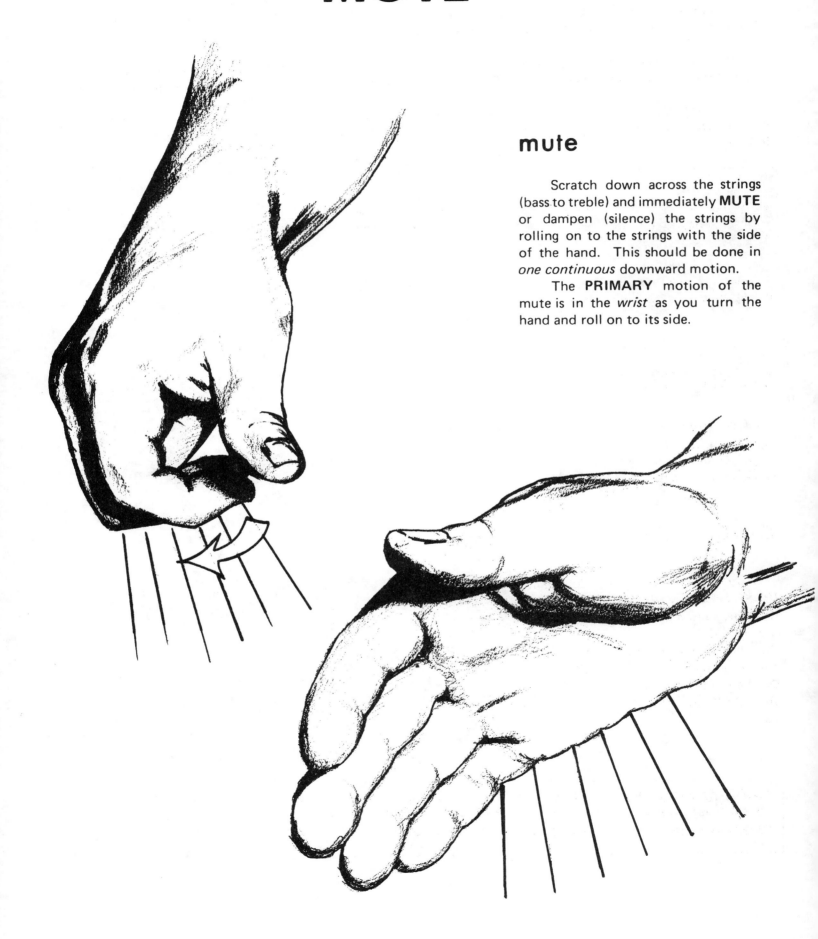

## mute

Scratch down across the strings (bass to treble) and immediately **MUTE** or dampen (silence) the strings by rolling on to the strings with the side of the hand. This should be done in *one continuous* downward motion.

The **PRIMARY** motion of the mute is in the *wrist* as you turn the hand and roll on to its side.

# folk strums

Although a variety of methods exist, strumming or plucking the guitar falls into two general categories: 1. pick-style and, 2. finger-style. Both are applicable to many styles of music.

In the pick-style, the guitar is strummed with a flat pick (plectrum) that is held between the thumb and index finger of the hand. Using a down-stroke, an up-stroke, or a combination of the two, a variety of strums are possible.

In the finger-style, the guitar strums are performed with the thumb and first three fingers of the right hand. This is done with or without the use of finger picks. The finger-style method is widely used as an accompaniment for folk songs.

NOTE: For the beginner, finger picks are not recommended. Shape the nails of the right hand to the contour of the fleshy part of the finger. The nails should not extend further than 1/16 inch beyond the fingers.

There are two types of finger-style strums: 1. folk strums — brushes, sweeps and scratches; 2. finger plucks — plucks, pinches, pulls and arpeggios.

## brush strums

Brush (strum) down across the strings (low to high) with the backs of the index and middle fingers (nails) of the right hand while holding the chord with the left hand. fig. 1

## thumb brush

Every chord is built upon a foundation or root (R). It is the root of the chord that gives the chord its name; thus, a D chord has a D as its root. In the thumb/brush strum, the thumb plucks the root of the chord followed by the fingers (index and middle) brushing the top four strings (low to high). On the third beat of the measure, the thumb may alternate to the fifth (5) of the chord (optional). fig. 2

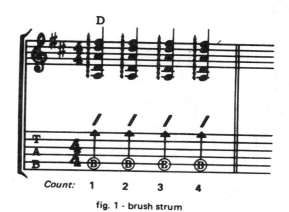

fig. 1 - brush strum

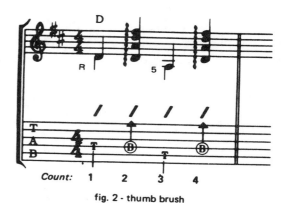

fig. 2 - thumb brush

NOTE: Strums are suggested for each of the songs of this book. Always practice the chords first with a simple brush strum as you learn the melody and chords of the song. Having learned the song and chords, practice the suggested strum until it is "grooved." Now, put it together.

# thumb sweep in 3/4

The thumb plucks the root (R) of the chord and then continues to sweep the rest of the strings in the chord (low to high). For example, in the E chord the thumb plucks the 6th string (R) and then sweeps down across the 4th, 3rd, 2nd, and 1st strings. fig. 3

In the A chord, the thumb plucks the 5th string (R) and then sweeps down across the 4th, 3rd, 2nd and 1st strings.

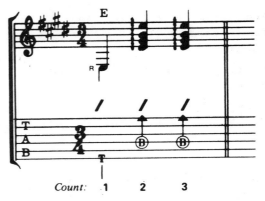

fig. 3 - thumb sweep in 3/4

# sweep scratch

The SWEEP SCRATCH strum uses two right hand techniques: (1) Sweep — the thumb sweeps down across all the strings in the chord; (2) Scratch — the index finger scratches an up-down-up pattern. fig. 4

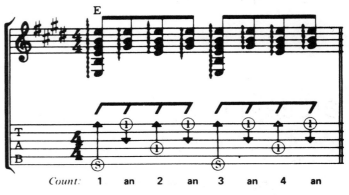

fig. 4 - sweep scratch

# syncopated strum

The SYNCOPATED STRUM uses two right hand techniques — the brush and the scratch (up). It is the rhythm of the strum that is new; it is a syncopated rhythm in that the beat receiving the greatest emphasis is an up-beat. The first scratch (up) is played on the up-beat (2 an) and should be accented or stressed. fig. 5

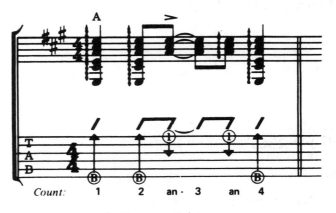

fig. 5 - syncopated strum

RHYTHM — Syncopation is the shifting of emphasis from what is ordinarily the strong beat (downbeat) to emphasis on the weak beat (up-beat). This is often done by tying notes together.

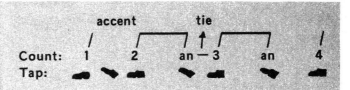

# finger plucks

Finger-style folk guitar is closely related in right hand technique to flamenco and classic styles of playing the guitar.

*p* = thumb (pulgar)   *m* = middle (medico)
*i* = index (indice)   *a* = ring (anular)

## hand position

The thumb is straight and rigid (not bent) and extends beyond the fingers toward the middle of the sound hole. Place the fingers on the strings as follows:
1. index finger on the 3rd string (G)
2. middle finger on the 2nd string (B)
3. ring finger on the 1st string (E) fig. 6

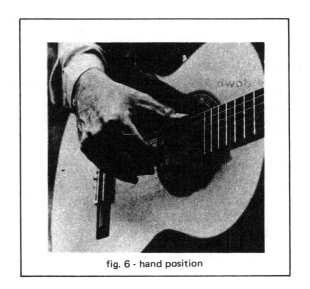

fig. 6 - hand position

## arpeggio - 3/4

An arpeggio is a broken chord strum; that is, the notes (strings) are plucked one after the other. With the right hand in the proper position, the thumb plucks the root (R) of the chord and the fingers pluck the strings individually. fig. 7

fig. 7 - arpeggio - 3/4

## arpeggio - 4/4

The thumb plucks the root (R) of the chord. Keep the hand relaxed. Use a finger motion instead of hand, wrist or arm motion. Do not lift the palm of the hand. Keep the thumb rigid. fig. 8

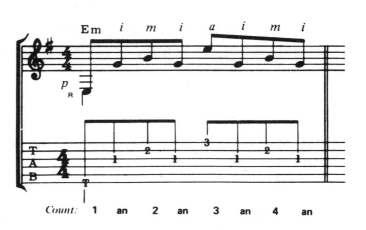

fig. 8 - arpeggio - 4/4

# thumb pluck 3/4

In the THUMB PLUCK strum, the thumb plucks the root (R) of the chord followed by the fingers plucking the treble strings upward and inward. **fig. 9**

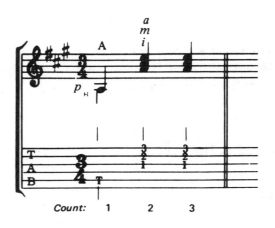

fig. 9 - thumb pluck 3/4

# thumb pluck 4/4

Alternating the thumb between the root (R) of the chord and the fifth (5) is optional at this point. You may simplify the strum by omitting the alternating bass pattern. **fig. 10**

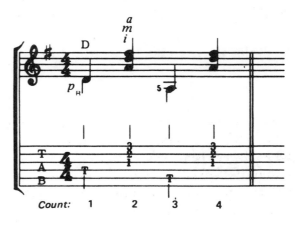

fig. 10 - thumb pluck 4/4

# thumb pluck/variation in 4/4

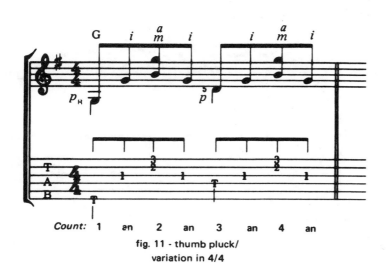

fig. 11 - thumb pluck/
variation in 4/4

# thumb pluck/variation in 3/4

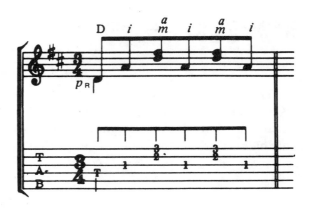

fig. 12 - thumb pluck /
variation in 3/4

# transposition

There are many vocal classifications. The choice of key for the guitarist is determined by his or her vocal range; that is, the distance between the lowest note you can sing and the highest note. You may occasionally need to transpose a song to a more suitable key in order to raise or lower the range.

There are two ways to transpose on the guitar:
1. with the use of a capo
2. by transposing to an entirely new key

## capo

A capo is a clamp device that when placed on the guitar neck shortens the string length and thus raises the pitch. Treating the capo as the nut of the guitar, you may continue to use easy open string chords typical of the folk/country/western style while raising the vocal range of the song.

Chords played in the key of A with the capo at the first fret would sound in the key of Bb. Chords played in the key of G with the capo at the third fret would also sound in the key of Bb. By placing the capo at the third fret and playing in the key of C, it is possible to sound in the key of Eb.

*Elastic, spring and stirrup capo*

The following chart will help you identify the name of the new key, fig. 1

| CHORDS played in these KEYS | WILL SOUND CHORDS in these KEYS when the CAPO is placed at the following FRETS: | | | | |
|---|---|---|---|---|---|
| | 1 | 2 | 3 | 4 | 5 |
| A | Bb | B | C | Db | D |
| C | Db | D | Eb | E | F |
| D | Eb | E | F | Gb | G |
| E | F | Gb | G | Ab | A |
| F | Gb | G | Ab | A | Bb |
| G | Ab | A | Bb | B | C |

fig. 1

# DOWN BY THE STATION

**Traditional**

**CHORDS USED IN THIS SONG:**  **SUGGESTED STRUM:**

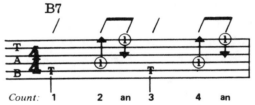

*Count:* 1  2 an  3  4 an

Thumb Scratch variation: thumb plucks the root
(R) of the chord; optional — thumb plucks the fifth
fifth (5) of the chord on 3.

Down by the sta - tion ear - ly in the morn - ing,

See the lit - tle puf - fer - bil - lies all in a row. See the sta - tion mas - ter

pull the lit - tle han - dle. Choo! Choo! Poof! Poof! Off they go.

© Copyright 1976, Belwin-Mills Publishing Corp.

# GOOD MORNING, MISTER RAILROADMAN

**Traditional**

**CHORDS USED IN THIS SONG:**                **SUGGESTED STRUM:**

Count: 1   2   3

**Thumb Brush strum:** thumb plucks the root (R) of the chord; fingers brush down across the strings.

**First Note**    Moderate

D

"Good morn - ing Mis - ter Rail - road ___ man.
It's nine - six - teen and two - for - ty

G                                  D

man. What time do your trains ___ roll by? _____ At
four, Twen - ty - five min - utes till five. _____ Thank

G                                  D

nine - six - teen and two - for - ty - four And
you, Mis - ter two Rail - road man. I

A7                                 D

twen - ty - five min - utes till five. _____
want to watch your trains roll by." _____

© Copyright 1976, Belwin-Mills Publishing Corp.

# ROW, ROW, ROW YOUR BOAT

Round

**CHORDS USED IN THIS SONG:**

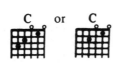

C or C

**SUGGESTED STRUM:**

*Count:* 1    2

Brush strum: index and middle fingers strum down-ward across the strings.

Lively

**First Note**

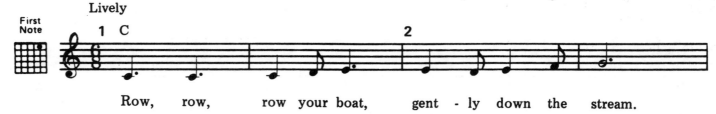

1 C        2

Row,    row,    row your boat,    gent - ly down the stream.

3        4

Mer - ri - ly, mer - ri - ly, mer - ri - ly, mer - ri - ly, life is but a dream.

# LONDON STREET

Traditional

**CHORDS USED IN THIS SONG:**

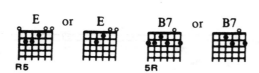

E or E    B7 or B7

R5        5R

**SUGGESTED STRUM:**

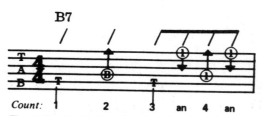

B7

*Count:* 1    2    3   an   4   an

**Thumb Brush variation:** thumb plucks the root (R) of the chord; optional — thumb plucks the fifth (5) of the chord on 3.

Moderately

**First Note**

E        B7    E

1. As    I went o - ver Lon - don Street,    Lon - don Street, Lon-don Street, As

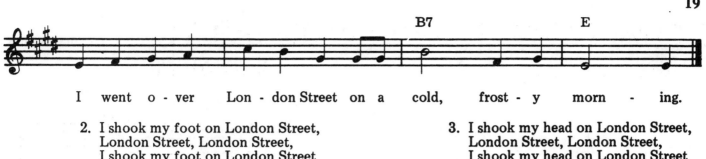

I went o - ver Lon - don Street on a cold, frost - y morn - ing.

2. I shook my foot on London Street,
London Street, London Street,
I shook my foot on London Street
On a cold, frosty morning.

3. I shook my head on London Street,
London Street, London Street,
I shook my head on London Street
On a cold, frosty morning.

# HICKORY, DICKORY, DOCK

Mother Goose

CHORDS USED IN THIS SONG:

SUGGESTED STRUM:

Brush strum: index and middle fingers strum downward across the strings.

Brightly

Hick - o - ry, dick - o - ry dock,___ The mouse ran up the clock. ___ The clock struck "one", The mouse ran down, Hick - o - ry, dick - o - ry dock. _____

# LOVE SOMEBODY (Yes I Do)

English Folk Song

**CHORDS USED IN THIS SONG:**

**SUGGESTED STRUM:**

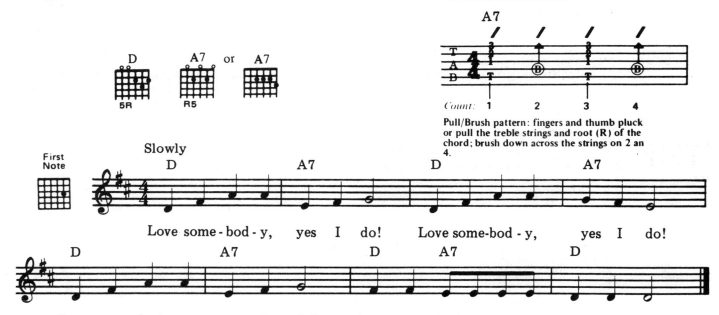

Pull/Brush pattern: fingers and thumb pluck or pull the treble strings and root (R) of the chord; brush down across the strings on 2 and 4.

Love some-bod - y, yes I do! Love some-bod - y, yes I do!

Love some - bod - y, yes I do! Love some - bod - y but I won't tell who.

2. Love somebody, can't guess who!
   Love somebody, can't guess who!
   Love somebody, can't guess who!
   Love somebody but I won't tell who!

3. Love somebody, yes I do!
   Love somebody, yes I do!
   Love somebody, could be you!
   Hope somebody loves me too!

# THE CENTIPEDE AND THE FROG

**Traditional**

**CHORDS USED IN THIS SONG:**

**SUGGESTED STRUM:**

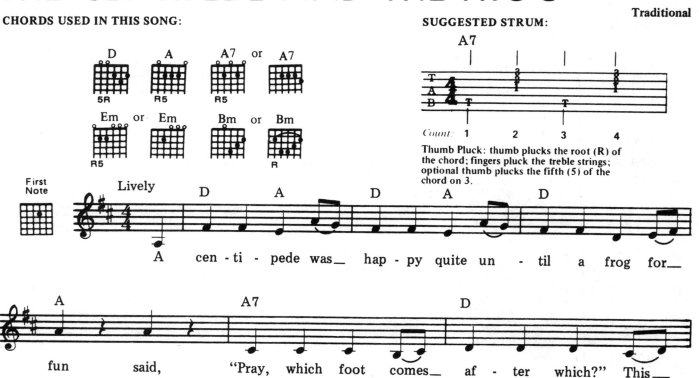

Thumb Pluck: thumb plucks the root (R) of the chord; fingers pluck the treble strings; optional thumb plucks the fifth (5) of the chord on 3.

A cen - ti - pede was_ hap - py quite un - til a frog for_

fun said, "Pray, which foot comes_ af - ter which?" This_

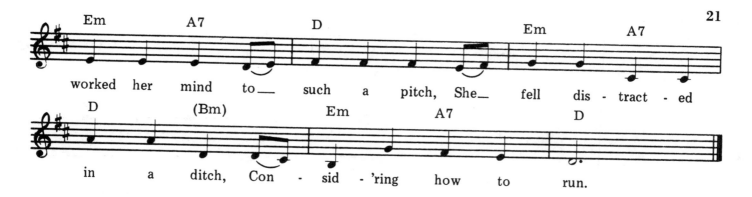

worked her mind to__ such a pitch, She__ fell dis - tract - ed

in a ditch, Con - sid - 'ring how to run.

# THE HUNTING HORN

**CHORDS USED IN THIS SONG:**

**SUGGESTED STRUM:**

Round

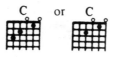

C or C

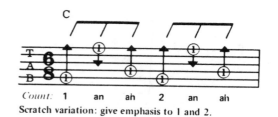

Count: 1 an ah 2 an ah
Scratch variation: give emphasis to 1 and 2.

Lively
**1** C

Mer - ri - ly, mer - ri - ly greet the morn,

**2**

Cheer - i - ly, cheer - i - ly sound the horn:

**3**

Hark to the ech - o hear it play O'er

**4**

hill and dale and far a - way.

# WHO DID SWALLOW JONAH?

**Traditional**

**CHORDS USED IN THIS SONG:**

**SUGGESTED STRUM:**

Who did swal - low Jo - nah down?

2. The whale did, whale did, whale did
   whale did.  The whale did swallow } *3 times*
   Jo-Jo-Jonah
   The whale did swallow Jonah,
     the whale did swallow Jonah
   The whale did swallow Jonah, up!

3. Noah, Noah, Noah, Noah } *3 times*
   Noah in the ark, ark, arky
   Noah in the arky, Noah in the ark,
   Noah in the arky, bailed!

4. Daniel, Daniel, Daniel, Daniel, } *3 times*
   Daniel in the li-li-li-on
   Daniel in the lion, Daniel in the lion
   Daniel in the lion's den!

5. David, David, David, David, } *3 times*
   David killed Goli-li-liath
   David killed Goliath, David killed Goliath,
   David killed Goliath, dead!

# ONE MEAT BALL

**CHORDS USED IN THIS SONG:**

Traditional

**SUGGESTED STRUM:**

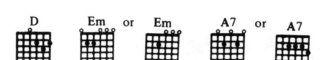

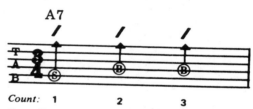

Count: 1   2   3

Sweep/Brush strum: thumb sweeps downward:
fingers brush downward.

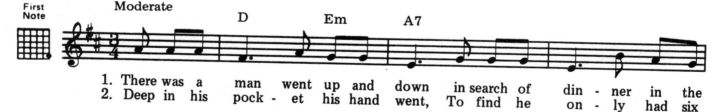

1. There was a man went up and down in search of din - ner in the
2. Deep in his pock - et his hand went, To find he on - ly had six

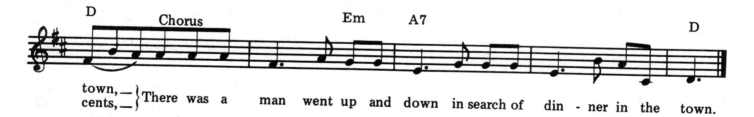

town, —}
cents, —} There was a man went up and down in search of din - ner in the town.

3. He found at last the cheapest place,
   And entered it with anxious face *(Chorus)*

4. The cheapest offer of them all
   Was "Twelve cents for two meat balls" *(Chorus)*

5. The waiter aksed him for his call,
   He whispered gently, "One meat ball!" *(Chorus)*

6. The waiter roared it through the hall,
   The guests all heard his "One meat ball" *(Chorus)*

7. The young man said, not quite at ease,
   "A piece of bread sir, if you please." *(Chorus)*

8. The waiter roared, once more with gall,
   "You get no bread with one meat ball!" *(Chorus)*

# AH, POOR BIRD

Round

**CHORDS USED IN THIS SONG:**

**SUGGESTED STRUM:**

*Count:* 1    2    3    4

Sweep strum: thumb strums downward across the strings.

Ah, poor bird, take thy flight,

Far a - bove the shad - ows of this sad night.

# GO IN AND OUT THE WINDOW

Traditional

**CHORDS USED IN THIS SONG:**

**SUGGESTED STRUM:**

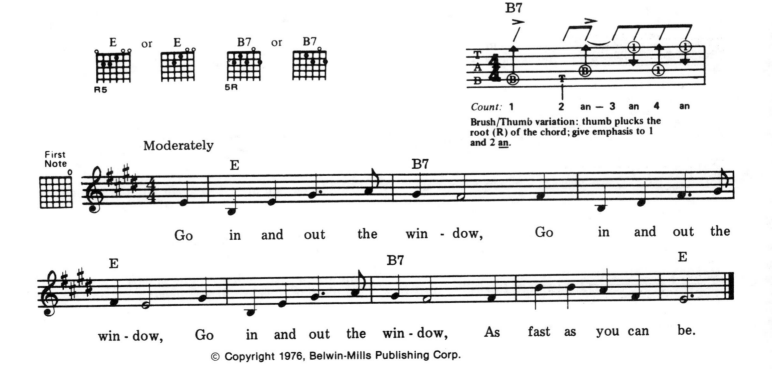

*Count:* 1    2 an — 3 an   4 an

Brush/Thumb variation: thumb plucks the root (R) of the chord; give emphasis to 1 and 2 an.

Go in and out the win - dow, Go in and out the

win - dow, Go in and out the win - dow, As fast as you can be.

# THE SPIDER AND THE FLY

Traditional

**CHORDS USED IN THIS SONG:**

**SUGGESTED STRUM:**

D    A7  or  A7    G  or  G

A7

Count:  1    2

Thumb Brush strum: thumb plucks the root (R)
of the chord; fingers brush downward.

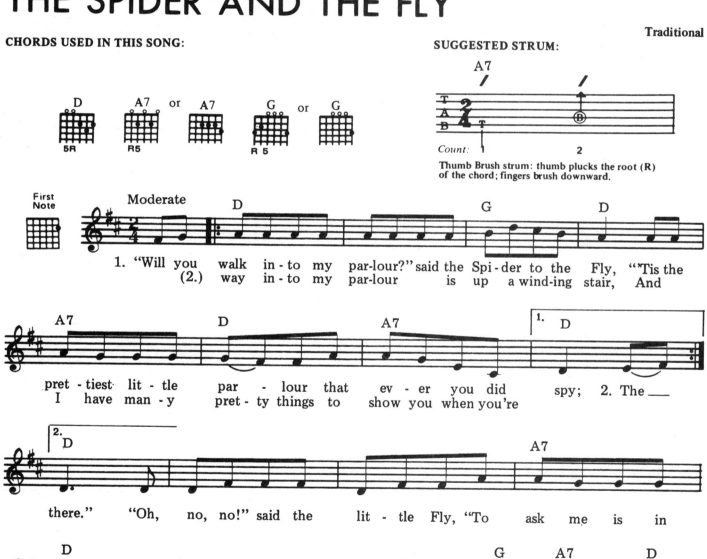

First Note — Moderate

D      G      D

1. "Will you walk in-to my par-lour?" said the Spi-der to the Fly, "'Tis the
(2.) way in-to my par-lour is up a wind-ing stair, And

A7      D      A7      **1.** D

pret-tiest lit-tle par-lour that ev-er you did spy; 2. The___
I have man-y pret-ty things to show you when you're

**2.** D

there."  "Oh, no, no!" said the lit-tle Fly, "To ask me is in

D      G   A7   D

vain.  For who goes up your wind-ing stair shall ne'er come down a-gain."

# THE FOX

**CHORDS USED IN THIS SONG:**

SUGGESTED STRUM:

TRADITIONAL

**Brightly**

Fox went out one chil - ly night.

Prayed for the moon to give him light, for he'd man-y a mile to

do that night be - fore he'd reach the town. Oh,

town oh, town oh, Man - y a mile to

go that night be - fore he'd reach the town oh.

2. Well he ran till he came to a great big bin,
The ducks and geese were there put in.
He said "A couple of you are gonna grease my chin
Before I leave this town oh,
    Town oh, town oh,
A couple of you are gonna grease my chin
Before I leave this town oh."

3. Well he grabbed the grey goose by the neck
And he slung a duck across his back,
He didn't mind the quack, quack, quack,
Legs all danglin' down oh,
    Down oh, down oh,
He didn't mind the quack, quack, quack,
Legs all danglin' down.

4. Well old-a Mother Flipper Flopper jumped out of bed,
She ran to the window and she put out her head
She cried, "John, John, the grey goose is gone,
The fox is on the town oh,
    Town oh, town oh,
John, John, the grey goose is gone
The fox is on the town."

5. Well then John he ran up to the top of the hill,
He blowed his horn both loud and shrill,
The fox he said, "I better flee with the kill
Or they'll be on my trail oh,"
    Trail oh, trail oh,"
The fox he said, "I better flee with the kill
Or they'll be on my trail."

6. Well he ran till he came to his cozy den,
There were little ones, eight, nine, ten,
They said, "Daddy, better go back again
'Cause it must be a mighty fine town oh,
    Town oh, town oh,"
They said, "Daddy, better go back again
'Cause it must be a mighty fine town."

7. The fox and his wife, without any strife,
Cut up the goose with fork and knife,
They never had such a supper in their life
And the little ones chewed on the bones oh,
    Bones oh, bones oh,
They never had such a supper in their life
And the little ones chewed on the bones.

# NINE POUND HAMMER

**SPIRITUAL**

**CHORDS USED IN THIS SONG:**

**SUGGESTED STRUM:**

A    D    E7

A

Count: 1    2  an – 3  an  4

Syncopated strums: give emphasis to 2 an.

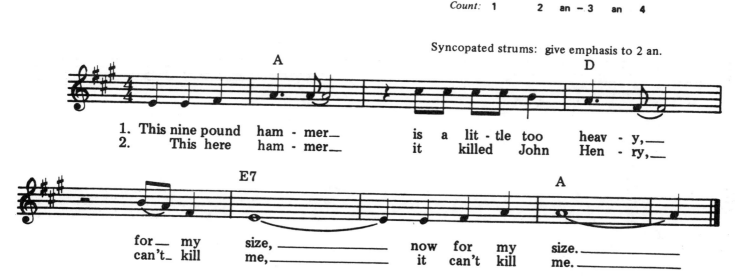

1. This nine pound ham - mer___ is a lit - tle too heav - y,___ for___ my size, _____ now for my size. _____

2.     This here ham - mer___ it killed John Hen - ry,___ can't_ kill me, _____ it can't kill me. _____

# COME FOLLOW

John Hilton

**CHORDS USED IN THIS SONG:**

**SUGGESTED STRUM:**

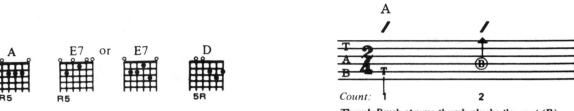

A     E7   or   E7     D

R5       R5             5R

Count:     1           2

**CAPO I: Key of B♭**

Thumb Brush strum: thumb plucks the root (R)
of the chord; fingers brush downward.

Moderate

Come fol - low, fol - low, fol - low, fol - low, fol - low, fol - low me.

Whith-er shall I fol - low, fol - low, fol - low, whith-er shall I fol - low, fol - low thee?

To the green - wood, to the green-wood, to the green - wood, green - wood tree!

# SOLFA CANON

**CHORDS USED IN THIS SONG:**

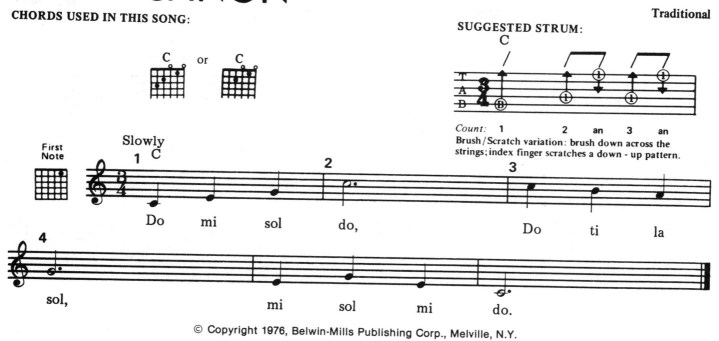

Count: 1    2   an   3   an
Brush/Scratch variation: brush down across the strings; index finger scratches a down - up pattern.

Slowly

Do mi sol do,    Do ti la

sol,      mi sol mi do.

# HEAVEN AND EARTH

**CHORDS USED IN THIS SONG:**

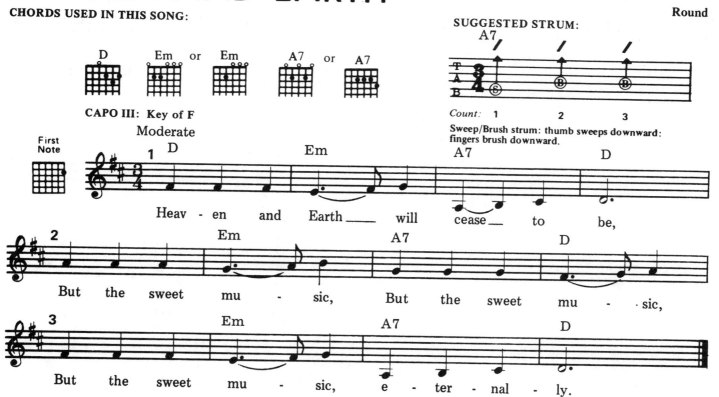

Count: 1    2    3
Sweep/Brush strum: thumb sweeps downward: fingers brush downward.

**CAPO III:** Key of F

Moderate

Heav - en and Earth ___ will cease ___ to be,

But the sweet mu - sic, But the sweet mu - sic,

But the sweet mu - sic, e - ter - nal - ly.

# SOURWOOD MOUNTAIN

Traditional

**CHORDS USED IN THIS SONG:**

**SUGGESTED STRUM:**

Count: 1 an 2 an 3 an 4 an

Thumb Scratch variation: thumb plucks the root (R) of the chord; scratch an up - down - up pattern.

**CAPO III: Key of F**

Moderato

1. Chick - en crow - ing on Sour - wood Moun - tain,
2. My true love is a blue - eyed dais - y,

Hi - dee - ing - di did - dy - i - day! So man - y pret - ty gals
Hi - dee - ing - di did - dy - i - day! If I don't get her I'll

I can't count 'em, Hi - dee - ing - di did - dy - i - day!
sure go cra - zy, Hi - dee - ing - di did - dy - i - day!

# MORNING IS COME

Round

**CHORDS USED IN THIS SONG:**

**SUGGESTED STRUM:**

Count: 1 2 an 3 an

Thumb Scratch variation: thumb plucks the root (R) of the chord; index finger scratches a down-up pattern.

Slowly

Morn - ing is come, Night is a - way,

Rise with the sun, And wel - come the day.

# ALPHABET SONG

Mother Goose

**CHORDS USED IN THIS SONG:**

**SUGGESTED STRUM:**

© Copyright 1976, Belwin-Mills Publishing Corp.

# I HAD A ROOSTER

**Traditional**

**CHORDS USED IN THIS SONG:**

A    E7  or  E7    D

CAPO I: Key of Bb

**SUGGESTED STRUM:**

Count:  1    2    3

Thumb Pluck: thumb plucks the root (R)
of the chord; fingers pluck the treble strings.

First Note

**Lively**

A

1. I had a roost-er and the roost-er pleased me. I
2. I had a cat ___ and the cat ___ pleased me. I
3. I had a pig ___ and the pig ___ pleased me. I
4. I had a cow ___ and the cow ___ pleased me. I
5. I had a ba-by and the ba-by pleased me. I

E7

fed ___ my roost-er on a green ber-ry tree. The
fed ___ my cat ___ on a green ber-ry tree. The
fed ___ my pig ___ on a green ber-ry tree. The
fed ___ my cow ___ on a green ber-ry tree. The
fed ___ my ba-by on a green ber-ry tree. The

A   *NOTE: Omit these FOUR BARS on 1st verse only*

lit - tle cat ___ went "meow, meow," the
lit - tle pig ___ went "oink, oink," the
lit - tle cow ___ went "moo, moo," the
lit - tle ba-by went "waaagh, waaagh," the

D

lit - tle roost-er went "cock - a - doo-dle - doo, dee

A       D       E7       A

doo-dle-dee doo-dle-dee doo-dle-dee doo."

# SHORTNIN' BREAD

**Traditional**

**CHORDS USED IN THIS SONG:**

**SUGGESTED STRUM:**

Thumb Brush variation: thumb plucks the root (R) of the chord; fingers brush down across the strings; optional — thumb plucks the fifth (5) of the chord on 3.

Put on the skil-let, __ put on the lid, Mam-my's gon-na make a lit-tle short-nin' bread. That ain't all she's gon-na do, Mam-my's gon-na make a lit-tle cof-fee too. Mam-my's lit-tle ba-by loves short-nin', short-nin', Mam-my's lit-tle ba-by loves short-nin' bread. Mam-my's lit-tle ba-by loves short-nin', short-nin', Mam-my's lit-tle ba-by loves short-nin' bread.

* optional

# BILL GROGGIN'S GOAT

**Traditional**

**CHORDS USED IN THIS SONG:**

**SUGGESTED STRUM:**

*Count:* 1  2  an – 3  an  4
Syncopated strum: give emphasis to the accented
beat – 2 an.

There was a man (there was a man) Now please take note (now please take

note) There was a man (there was a man) Who had a goat (who had a

goat) He loved that goat (he loved that goat) In - deed he did (in - deed he

did) He loved the goat (he loved that goat) Just like a kid. (just like a kid.)

2. One day that goat, felt frisk and fine;
   Ate three red shirts, right off the line.
   The man, he grabbed, him by the back,
   And tied him to a railroad track.

3. Now, when that train, hove into sight,
   That goat grew pale, and green with fright.
   He heaved a sigh, as if in pain;
   Coughed up the shirts, and flagged the train.

# ANIMAL FAIR

**CHORDS USED IN THIS SONG:**

**SUGGESTED STRUM:**

**Traditional**

Scratch variation: give emphasis to 1 and 2.

Lively

I went to the an - i - mal fair, _____ The birds and beasts were there, _____ The big ba - boon, by the light of the moon was comb - ing his au - burn hair. _____ You ought to have seen the monk; _____ He sat on the el - e - phant's trunk, _____ The el - e - phant sneezed, and fell on his knees, And what be - came of the monk, the monk, the monk, the monk?

# WHERE WOULD YOU LIKE TO BE?

South African
Contributed by **ARTHUR BOOS**

**CHORDS USED IN THIS SONG:**

A   E7  or  E7

**CAPO I: Key of B♭**

**SUGGESTED STRUM:**

Count: 1 an 2 an 3 an 4 an

Rumba pattern: thumb plucks the root (R) of the chord or may alternate to the fifth (5) or 2 an and 4: give emphasis on 1, 2 an and 4.

First Note

Slowly

**A**
Ask me where I'd like to be, _____
*(Where would you like to be?)*

**E7**
Ask me where I'd like to be, _____ I've
*(Where would you like to be?)*

**A**
giv - en it a lot of thought my an - swer must be right. _____

**A**  **E7**  **A**
Sit - tin' by the bright fire light. _____

# IT AIN'T GONNA RAIN NO MO'

**CHORDS USED IN THIS SONG:**

Folk Song

© Copyright 1976, Belwin-Mills Publishing Corp., Melville, N.Y.

# WHO ARE YOU?

**Traditional**

**CHORDS USED IN THIS SONG:**

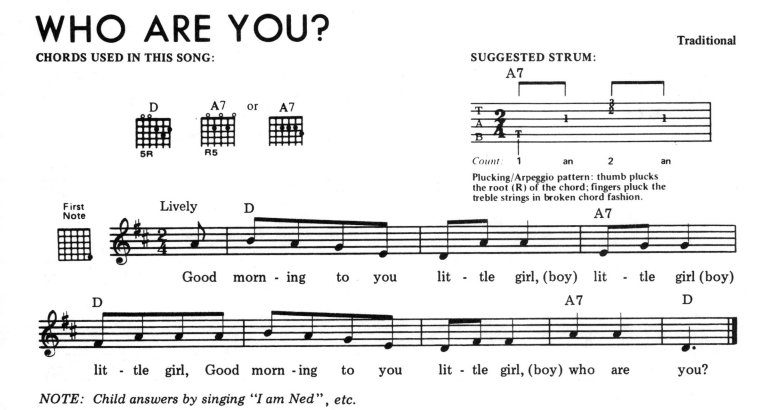

*NOTE: Child answers by singing "I am Ned", etc.*

© Copyright 1976, Belwin-Mills Publishing Corp.

# SARASPONDA

Dutch

**CHORDS USED IN THIS SONG:**

**SUGGESTED STRUM:**

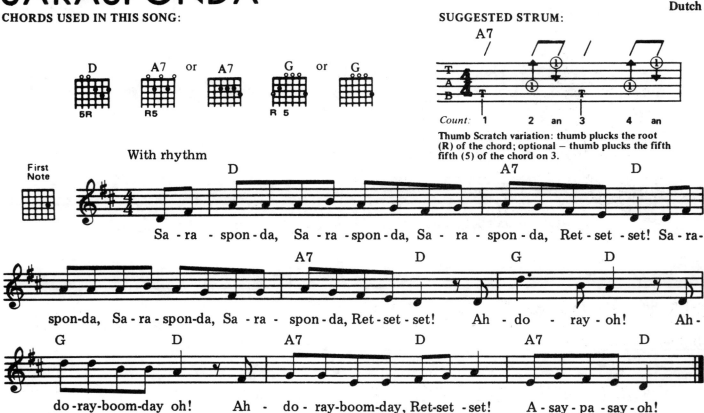

*Count:* 1    2 an 3    4 an

Thumb Scratch variation: thumb plucks the root
(R) of the chord; optional — thumb plucks the fifth
fifth (5) of the chord on 3.

With rhythm

Sa - ra - spon-da, Sa - ra - spon-da, Sa - ra - spon-da, Ret - set - set! Sa-ra-

spon-da, Sa - ra - spon-da, Sa - ra - spon-da, Ret - set - set! Ah - do - ray - oh! Ah -

do - ray-boom-day oh! Ah - do - ray-boom-day, Ret-set - set! A - say - pa - say - oh!

*NOTE:* A second part may be developed by having some children sing "boom-da" on the
D below the staff. Use an eighth note pattern.

# THE LITTLE BELLS OF WESTMINSTER

Traditional

**CHORDS USED IN THIS SONG:**

**SUGGESTED STRUM:**

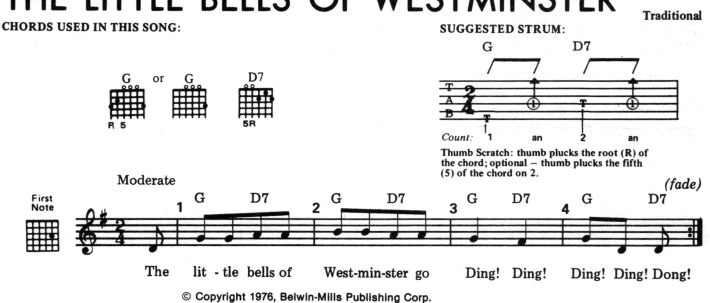

*Count:* 1 an 2 an

Thumb Scratch: thumb plucks the root (R) of
the chord; optional — thumb plucks the fifth
(5) of the chord on 2.

Moderate

(fade)

The lit - tle bells of West-min-ster go Ding! Ding! Ding! Ding! Dong!

# PITY THE POOR POTAT

South African
Contributed by **ARTHUR BOOS**

**CHORDS USED IN THIS SONG:**

**SUGGESTED STRUM:**

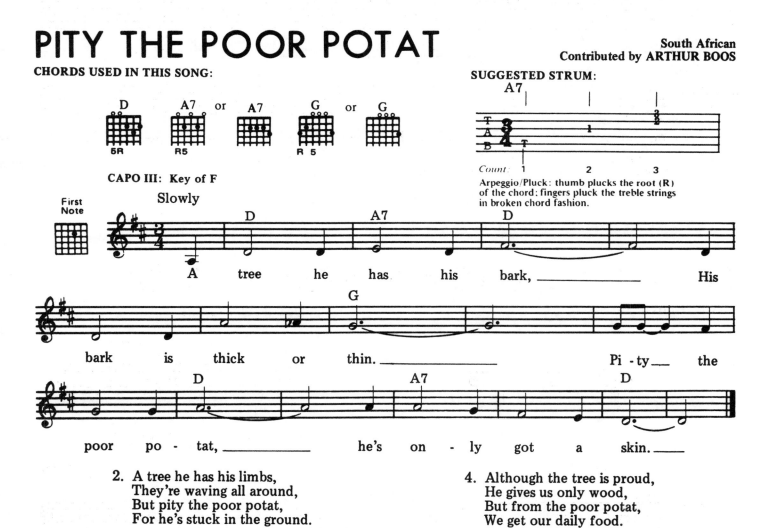

**CAPO III: Key of F**

A tree he has his bark, _____ His bark is thick or thin. _____ Pi - ty __ the poor po - tat, _____ he's on - ly got a skin. ___

2. A tree he has his limbs,
   They're waving all around,
   But pity the poor potat,
   For he's stuck in the ground.

3. The tree he has his leaves,
   There gazing in the sky,
   But pity the poor potat
   He can't see with his eyes.

4. Although the tree is proud,
   He gives us only wood,
   But from the poor potat,
   We get our daily food.

*NOTE: Pronounce potat (pay-tot).*
*It means potato.*

# OLD ABRAM BROWN

Round

**CHORDS USED IN THIS SONG:**

**SUGGESTED STRUM:**

*Count:* 1 an 2 an

Thumb Scratch: thumb plucks the root (R) of the chord; optional — thumb plucks the fifth (5) of the chord on 2.

Slowly

Old A - bram Brown is dead and gone,

We'll nev - er see hee more.

He used to wear an old grey coat,

All but - toned down be - fore.

# OFF TO BED, NOW

Traditional

**CHORDS USED IN THIS SONG:**

**SUGGESTED STRUM**

A7

*Count:* 1 2 3

Pull/Brush pattern: fingers and thumb pluck or pull the treble strings and root (R) of the chord; brush down across the strings on 2 an 3.

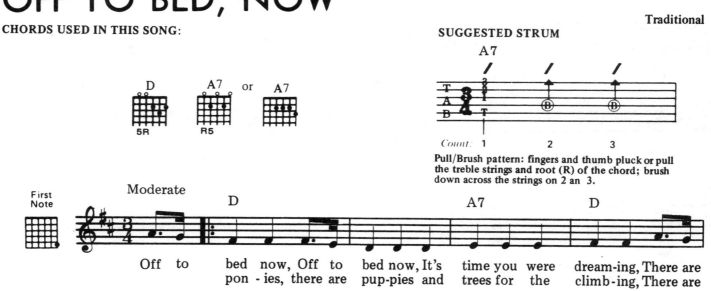

Moderate

D                                      A7            D

Off to bed now, Off to bed now, It's time you were dream-ing, There are
pon - ies, there are pup-pies and trees for the climb-ing, There are

friends that a - wait you to play un - til dawn. — There are
lawns and white pil - lows, and sil - ver - y songs.

# TINGA LAYO

**CHORDS USED IN THIS SONG:**

West Indies

Tin - ga La - yo, come, lit - tle don - key come,

Tin - ga La - yo, come, lit - tle don - key come.

My don - key walk, my don - key talk, my don - key eat with a knife and

fork. Tin - ga La - yo, come lit - tle don - key come, Tin - ga

La - yo, come lit - tle don - key come.

# HOOSEN JOHNNY

Folk Song

**CHORDS USED IN THIS SONG:**

**SUGGESTED STRUM:**

Thumb Scratch: thumb plucks the root (R) of the chord; optional — thumb plucks the fifth (5) of the chord on 2.

**CAPO I: Key of F**

Lively

The lit - tle black bull came down the mead-ow, Hoo - sen John - ny,

Hoo-sen John-ny, The lit - tle black bull came down the mea-dow Long time a - go.

Long time a - go, Long time a - go, The

lit - tle black bull came down the mead-ow, Long time a - go.

2. First he pawed and then he bellowed,
Hoosen Johnny, Hoosen Johnny
First he pawed and then he bellowed,
Long time ago.
Long time ago, long time ago,
First he'd paw the then he'd bellow,
Long time ago.

3. He whet his horn on a white oak sapling.
Hoosen Johnny, (etc.)

4. He shook his tail, he jarred the river.
Hoosen Johnny, (etc.)

5. He paw the dirt in the heifers' faces,
Hoosen Johnny, (etc.)

*\* NOTE: Chords in parenthesis may be omitted.*

© Copyright 1976, Belwin-Mills Publishing Corp.

# FATHER'S WHISKERS

**CHORDS USED IN THIS SONG:**

Traditional

**SUGGESTED STRUM:**

A

*Count:* 1  2  an  3  an  4

Thumb Scratch variation: thumb plucks the root (R) of the chord; optional — thumb plucks the fifth (5) of the chord on 3.

A        E7    or    E7       D

R5        R5              5R

First Note

Moderate

A                                                E7

I have a dear old dad-dy, for whom I night-ly pray. He

A          Chorus

has a set of whis-kers that are al-ways in the way. They're al-ways in the way, The

D                    E7                                       A

cows eat them for hay. They hide the dirt on dad-dy's shirt, They're al-ways in the way.

2. Father had a strong back,
Now it's all caved in,
He stepped upon his whiskers,
And walked up to his chin. *(Chorus)*

3. Father has a daughter,
Her name is Ella Mae,
She climbs up father's whiskers
And braids them all the way. *(Chorus)*

4. Around the supper table,
We make a merry group,
Until dear father's whiskers,
Get tangled in the soup. *(Chorus)*

5. Father fought in Flanders,
He wasn't killed, you see,
His whiskers looked like bushes
And fooled the enemy. *(Chorus)*

# SLEEP, BABY, SLEEP

**Traditional**

**CHORDS USED IN THIS SONG:**

**SUGGESTED STRUM:**

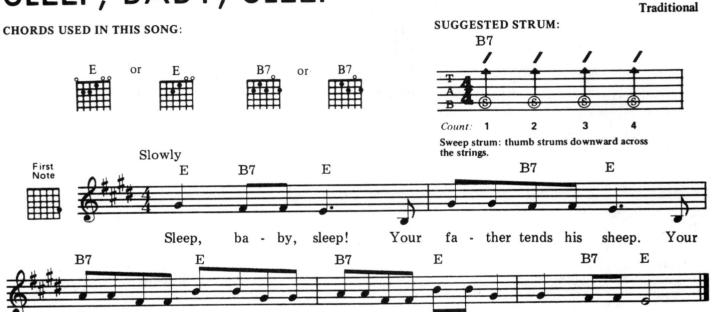

Sleep, ba - by, sleep! Your fa - ther tends his sheep. Your

moth - er shakes the dream-land tree, down falls a lit - tle dream for thee. Sleep, ba - by sleep!

# BAA, BAA, BLACK SHEEP

**Mother Goose**

**CHORDS USED IN THIS SONG:**

**SUGGESTED STRUM:**

Baa, baa black sheep, Have you an - y wool? Yes, sir,

**D**    **A7**    **D**    **G**

yes, sir, Three bags full; One for the mas - ter and one for the

**D**    **A7**    **D**    **A7**    **D**

dame, But none for the lit - tle boy who lives down the lane.

# MARY HAD A LITTLE LAMB

**CHORDS USED IN THIS SONG:**

Mother Goose

**SUGGESTED STRUM:**

A7

Pull/Brush pattern: fingers and thumb pluck or pull the treble strings and root (R) of the chord; brush down across the strings on 2 an 4.

First Note    Moderate

**D**    **A7**    **D**

1. Mar - y had a lit - tle lamb,   lit - tle lamb,   lit - tle lamb,
2. Ev' - ry - where that Mar - y went,   Mar - y went,   Mar - y went,
3. Fol - lowed her to school one day,   school one day,   school one day,
4. Made the chil - dren laugh and play,   laugh and play,   laugh and play,

**A7**    **D**

Mar - y had a lit - tle lamb, it's fleece was white as snow.
Ev' - ry - where that Mar - y went the lamb was sure to go.
Fol - lowed her to school one day, which was a - gainst the rules.
Made the chil - dren laugh and play to see a lamb at school.

# IT'S HOW WE DRIVE THE WINTER OUT

Traditional

**CHORDS USED IN THIS SONG:**

**SUGGESTED STRUM:**

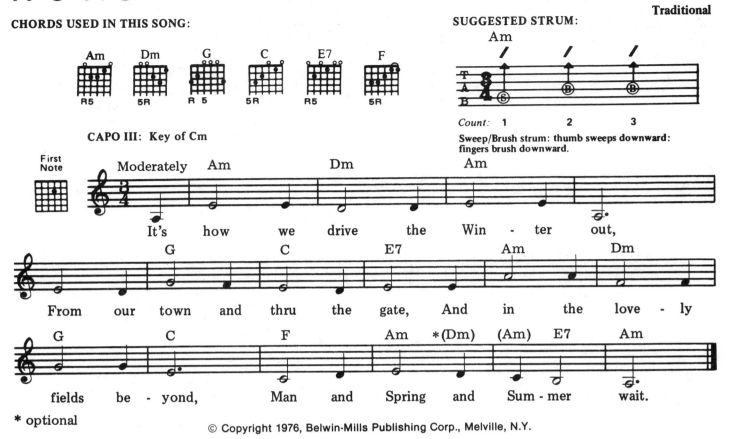

CAPO III: Key of Cm

*Sweep/Brush strum: thumb sweeps downward: fingers brush downward.*

First Note

Moderately

It's how we drive the Win-ter out,

From our town and thru the gate, And in the love-ly

fields be-yond, Man and Spring and Sum-mer wait.

\* optional

# LET EVERYONE

Game Song

**CHORDS USED IN THIS SONG:**

**SUGGESTED STRUM:**

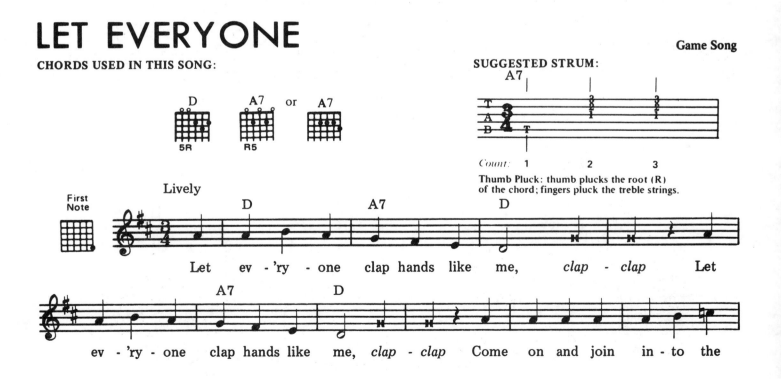

*Thumb Pluck: thumb plucks the root (R) of the chord; fingers pluck the treble strings.*

First Note

Lively

Let ev-'ry-one clap hands like me, *clap - clap* Let

ev-'ry-one clap hands like me, *clap - clap* Come on and join in-to the

game, *clap - clap* you'll find that it's al - ways the same. *clap - clap*

2. Let everyone stretch like me, etc.
3. Let everyone whistle like me, etc.
4. Let everyone yawn like me, etc.
5. Let everyone hiccough like me, etc.

6. Let everyone laugh like me, etc.
7. Let everyone stamp feet like me, etc.
8. Let everyone sneeze like me, etc.
9. Let everyone hee-haw like me, etc.

# HUMPTY DUMPTY

Mother Goose

CHORDS USED IN THIS SONG:

SUGGESTED STRUM:

*Count:* 1  2

Brush strum: index and middle fingers strum downward across the strings.

Lively

Hump - ty Dump - ty sat on a wall, Hump - ty Dump - ty had a great fall; All the king's hors - es and all the king's men, Could - n't put Hump - ty to - geth - er a - gain.

BAND AIDS

# THIS IS MY LITTLE HOUSE

**Traditional**

**CHORDS USED IN THIS SONG:**

**SUGGESTED STRUM:**

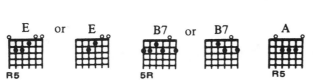

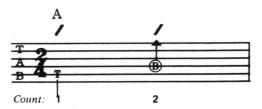

**Thumb Brush strum:** thumb plucks the root (R) of the chord; fingers brush downward.

**Moderato**

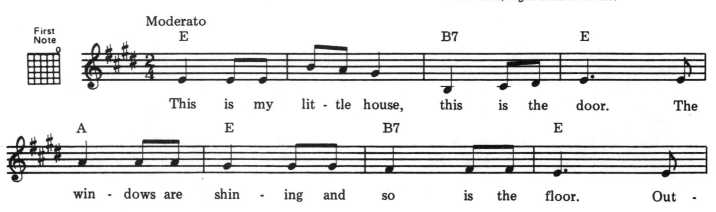

This is my lit - tle house, this is the door. The win - dows are shin - ing and so is the floor. Out -

side there is a chim - ney as tall as can be, with smoke that goes curl - ing up, Come and see.

# POLLY WOLLY DOODLE

**CHORDS USED IN THIS SONG:**

**SUGGESTED STRUM:**

Traditional

Thumb Pluck: thumb plucks the root (R) of the chord; fingers pluck the treble strings; optional thumb plucks the fifth (5) of the chord on 3.

Oh, I went down south for to see my Sal, Sing Pol - ly Wol - ly Doo-dle all the day; My Sal - ly am a spun - ky gal, Sing Pol - ly Wol - ly Doo - dle all the day. Fare thee well, Fare thee well, Fare thee well, my fai - ry fay. For I'm goin' to Loui - si - an - a, For to see my Su - si - an - na, Sing Pol - ly Wol - ly Doo - dle all the day.

EL 3052

# OLD KING COLE

Mother Goose

**CHORDS USED IN THIS SONG:**

**SUGGESTED STRUM:**

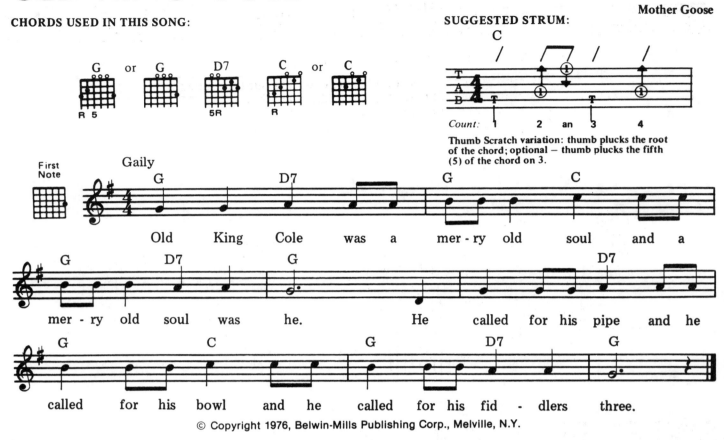

Thumb Scratch variation: thumb plucks the root of the chord; optional — thumb plucks the fifth (5) of the chord on 3.

Old King Cole was a mer-ry old soul and a
mer-ry old soul was he. He called for his pipe and he
called for his bowl and he called for his fid-dlers three.

# SING A SONG OF SIXPENCE

Mother Goose

**CHORDS USED IN THIS SONG:**

**SUGGESTED STRUM:**

Pull/Brush pattern: fingers and thumb pluck or pull the treble strings and root (R) of the chord; brush down across the strings on 2 an 4.

Sing a song of six - pence, A pock - et full of rye:
Four and twen - ty black birds baked in a pie. When the pie was o - pened the

birds be - gan to sing;   Was not that a dain - ty dish, to   set be - fore the king?

2. The king was in his counting house, counting out his money;
The queen was in the parlor, eating bread and honey.
The maid was in the garden, hanging out the clothes,
Along came a blackbird and snapped off her nose.

# SWEET BE YOUR SLEEP

**Traditional**

**CHORDS USED IN THIS SONG:**

**SUGGESTED STRUM:**

E or E   A   B7 or B7

Count:   1   2   3

Brush strum: index and middle fingers strum
downward across the strings.

First Note

**Slowly**

Good - night to you all   and sweet be your sleep;   May

an - gels a - round you their si - lent watch keep;   Good -

night,   good - night,   good - night,   good - night.

# OATS, PEAS, BEANS AND BARLEY GROW

**Traditional**

**CHORDS USED IN THIS SONG:**

**SUGGESTED STRUM:**

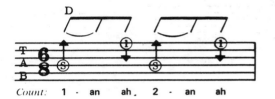

*Count:* 1 - an ah 2 - an ah

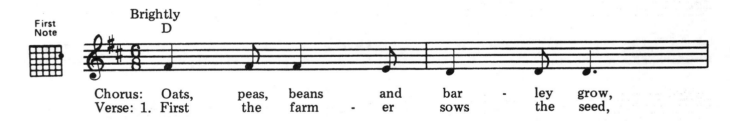

Chorus: Oats, peas, beans and bar - ley grow,
Verse: 1. First the farm - er sows the seed,

Oats, peas, beans and bar - ley grow, Can you and I or
Stands e - rect and takes his ease, He stamps his feet and

an - y - one know, How oats, peas, beans and bar - ley grow.
claps his hands, And turns a - round and views the land.

2. Next the farmer waters the seed,
Stands erect and takes his ease,
He stamps his foot and claps his hands
And turns around to view his lands. *(Chorus)*

3. Next the farmer harvests his seed,
Stands erect and takes his ease,
He stamps his foot and claps his hands
And turns around to view his lands. *(Chorus)*

# THREE LITTLE PIGGIES

**Traditional**

**CHORDS USED IN THIS SONG:**

**SUGGESTED STRUM:**

A    E7 or E7    D

R5    R5    R5    5R

**CAPO III: Key of C**

Count: 1    2    3

Thumb Pluck: thumb plucks the root (R)
of the chord; fingers pluck the treble strings.

First Note

Slowly    A    E7    A

1. Oh there once was a sow who had three lit - tle pigs,
2. Now one day one of the three lit - tle pigs, To the

E7    A

Three lit - tle pig - gies had she. _____ The
oth - er two pig - gies said he. _____ "Why

D    A

old sow al - ways went "oink, oink, oink," And the
don't we al - ways go "oink, oink, oink, It's so

E7    A

pig - gies went "wee, wee, wee - ee - ee." _____
child - ish to go wee, wee - ee - ee." _____

3. These three piggies grew skinny and lean,
   Skinny they well should be,
   For they always would try to go "oink, oink, oink,"
   And they wouldn't go "wee, wee, wee-ee-ee."

4. Now these three piggies then up and they died,
   So, don't ever try to go "oink, oink, oink,"
   When you oughta go "wee, wee, wee-ee-ee."

© Copyright 1976, Belwin-Mills Publishing Corp.

# CHOC'LATE CANDY

Traditional

**CHORDS USED IN THIS SONG:**

**SUGGESTED STRUM:**

*Count:* 1   2   an   3   an   4

**Thumb Scratch variation:** thumb plucks the root (R) of the chord; optional — thumb plucks the fifth (5) of the chord on 3.

1. Al-ly bal-ly, al-ly bal-ly bee, Sit-tin' on my dad-dy's knee,

Beg-ging for a wee pen-ny to buy some choc-'late can-dy.

2. Poor wee thing you're gettin' very thin,
A bundle of bones cov'red over with skin.
Now you're gettin' a wee double chin,
From suckin' choc'late candy.

3. Go to sleep now, my little man,
Seven o'clock and you playin's done.
Open your eyes to the morning sun,
And I'll give you some choc'late candy.

© Copyright 1976, Belwin-Mills Publishing Corp., Melville, N.Y.

# SWEETLY SINGS THE DONKEY

Round

**CHORDS USED IN THIS SONG:**

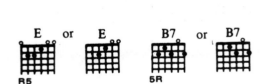

**SUGGESTED STRUM:**

*Count:* 1   2

**Thumb brush:** thumb plucks the root (R) of the chord.

Lively

Sweet-ly sings the don-key at the break of day.

© Copyright 1976, Belwin-Mills Publishing Corp.

If you don't sing loud - er, you will get no hay. _____

Hee - haw! Hee - haw! Hee - haw! Hee - haw! Hee - haw! _____

# HEY, DIDDLE DIDDLE

**CHORDS USED IN THIS SONG:**

Mother Goose

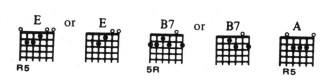

**SUGGESTED STRUM:**

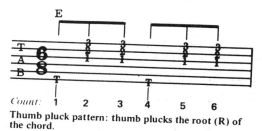

Thumb pluck pattern: thumb plucks the root (R) of the chord.

**First Note**

**Moderately**

Hey, did - dle did - dle, The cat and the fid - dle, The

cow jumped o - ver the moon; _____ The lit - tle dog laughed _ to

see such sport, And the dish ran a - way with the spoon. _____

© Copyright 1976, Belwin-Mills Publishing Corp.

# GREETINGS

**CHORDS USED IN THIS SONG:**

Traditional

A    D    E7    or    E7

R5    5R    R5

**SUGGESTED STRUM:**

A

Count: 1    2 an 3 an 4

Finger - Picking pattern: thumb alternates between the root (R) of the chord and the 3rd string; optional — thumb plucks the fifth (5) of the chord on 3.

**CAPO I: Key of B♭**

First Note

Moderate

A                    D                    A

Your_ right hand says "Good morn - ing, Good morn - ing" to

E7    A                    D        E7            A

you.    Your_ right hand says, "Good morn - ing, Good morn - ing" to you.

2. Your left hand says
   "Good day" * (wave it)

3. Your right foot says
   "Good evening" * (stamp it)

4. Your left foot says
   "Good night" * (stamp it)

5. Your right ear says
   "How are you?" * (cup it)

6. Your left ear says
   "I'm fine" * (cup it)

7. Your right eye says
   "How lovely" * (wink it)

8. Your left eye says
   "So pretty" * (wink it)

9. Your right nose says
   "It's sweet" * (grab the nose by
   the fingers and turn to the right)

10. Your left nose says
    "Let go of my nose!" * (grab the
    nose by the fingers while singing)

# THERE WAS AN OLD WOMAN
### (Who Lived In A Shoe)

Mother Goose

**CHORDS USED IN THIS SONG:**

SUGGESTED STRUM:

*Count:* 1 2 3 4

Sweep/Brush strum: thumb sweeps downward; fingers strum downward.

Em | or | Em | B7 | or | B7 | C | G

First Note

Moderate

**Em** ... **B7** ... **Em**

There was an old wom-an who lived ___ in a shoe. She

**C** ... **G** ... **D7** ... **G** ... **C**

had so man-y chil-dren she did-n't know what to do; She gave them some broth with-

**G** ... **B7** ... **Em** ... **C** ... **B7** ... **Em**

out an-y bread, And whipped them all sound-ly, and put ___ them to bed.

© Copyright 1976, Belwin-Mills Publishing Corp.

# THREE BLIND MICE

Mother Goose

**CHORDS USED IN THIS SONG:**

**SUGGESTED STRUM:**

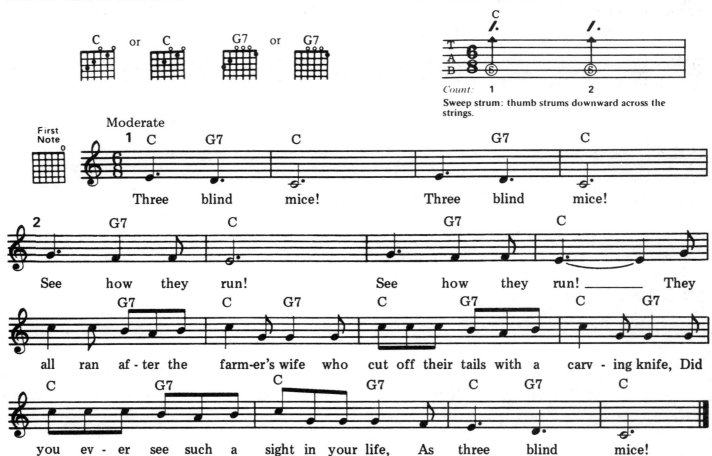

Count: 1   2

Sweep strum: thumb strums downward across the strings.

First Note

**Moderate**

**1** C   G7   C   G7   C

Three   blind   mice!   Three   blind   mice!

**2** G7   C   G7   C

See   how   they   run!   See   how   they   run! _____ They

G7   C   G7   C   G7   C   G7

all   ran   af-ter   the   farm-er's   wife   who   cut   off   their   tails   with   a   carv-ing   knife,   Did

C   G7   C   G7   C   G7   C

you   ev-er   see   such   a   sight   in   your   life,   As   three   blind   mice!

# BASAY DOWN

**West Indies Calypso**

**CHORDS USED IN THIS SONG:**

**SUGGESTED STRUM:**

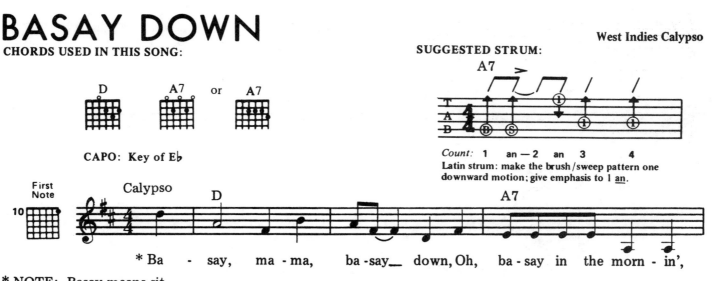

Count: 1   an — 2   an   3   4

Latin strum: make the brush/sweep pattern one downward motion; give emphasis to 1 an.

**CAPO: Key of E♭**

First Note

**Calypso**

D   A7

\* Ba - say,   ma - ma,   ba -say__ down, Oh,   ba - say   in   the   morn - in',

\* NOTE: Basay means sit

ba - say___ down. Ba - say down, Miss Mar - y, ba - say___ down, Ba - say

down, Miss Mar - y, ba - say___ down; Ba - say down, Miss Mar - y,

*D. C. al Fine*

ba - say___ down, Ba - say in the morn - in', ba - say___ down.

# LITTLE THINGS

**CHORDS USED IN THIS SONG:**

**SUGGESTED STRUM:**

**Traditional**

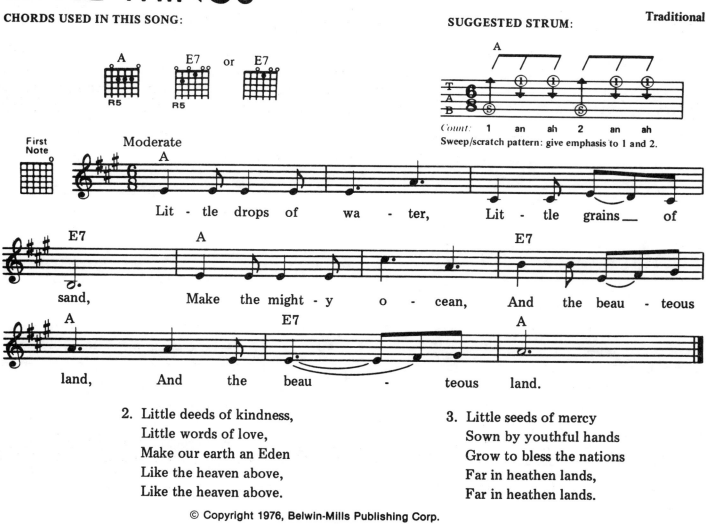

Count: 1 an ah 2 an ah
Sweep/scratch pattern: give emphasis to 1 and 2.

Lit - tle drops of wa - ter, Lit - tle grains___ of

sand, Make the might - y o - cean, And the beau - teous

land, And the beau - teous land.

2. Little deeds of kindness,
   Little words of love,
   Make our earth an Eden
   Like the heaven above,
   Like the heaven above.

3. Little seeds of mercy
   Sown by youthful hands
   Grow to bless the nations
   Far in heathen lands,
   Far in heathen lands.

60

# ALL THE PRETTY LITTLE HORSES

**Folk Song**
**Adapted by JERRY SNYDER**

Hush - a - by, don't you cry, go to sleep - y lit - tle ba - by.

When you wake, you shall have, all the pret - ty lit - tle hor - ses.

Blacks and bays, dap - ples and grays, Coach and six a - lit - tle hor - ses.

# WHITE SANDS AND GREY SANDS

**CHORDS USED IN THIS SONG:**

**SUGGESTED STRUM:**

**Traditional**

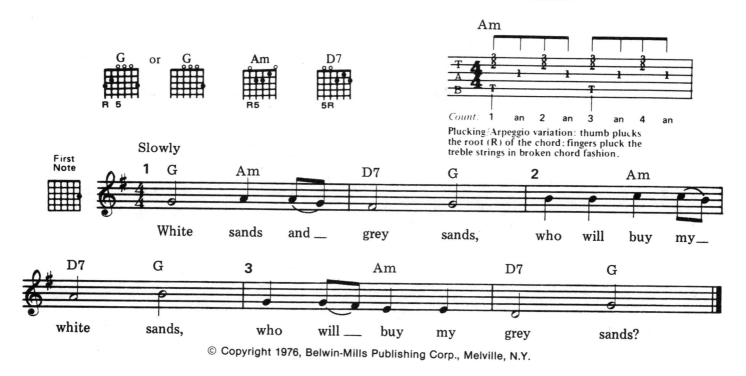

*Plucking/Arpeggio variation: thumb plucks the root (R) of the chord: fingers pluck the treble strings in broken chord fashion.*

White sands and __ grey sands, who will buy my __ white sands, who will __ buy my grey sands?

# CHARLEY OVER THE WATER

**CHORDS USED IN THIS SONG:**

**SUGGESTED STRUM:**

**Traditional**

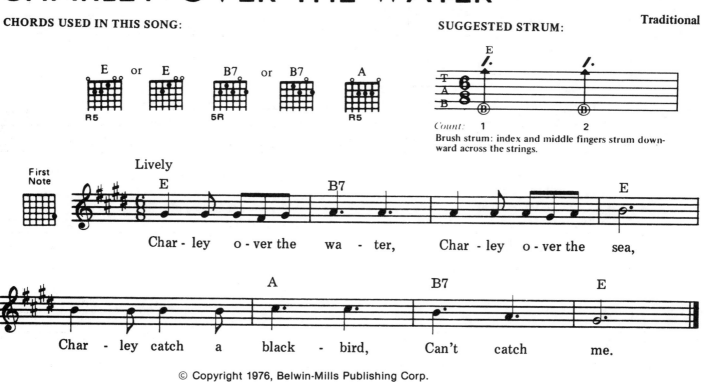

*Brush strum: index and middle fingers strum downward across the strings.*

Char - ley o - ver the wa - ter, Char - ley o - ver the sea,

Char - ley catch a black - bird, Can't catch me.

# JENNY JENKINS

**Traditional**

**CHORDS USED IN THIS SONG:**

**SUGGESTED STRUM:**

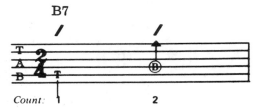

Thumb Brush strum: thumb plucks the root (R)
of the chord; fingers brush downward.

**Brightly**

Will you wear white, oh my dear, Oh my dear, Oh will you wear

white, Jen-ny Jen-kins? No, I won't wear

white, For the col-or's too bright. I'll buy me a fol-dy, rol-dy,

til-dy, tol-dy, seek a dou-ble, use a co-zy roll to find me.

Roll, Jen-ny Jen-kins roll.

2. Will you wear green, etc.
No, I won't wear green.
It's a shame to be seen.
*Chorus*

3. Will you wear yellow, etc.
No, I won't wear yellow,
For I'd never get a fellow.
*Chorus*

4. Will you wear brown, etc.
No, I won't wear brown.
For I'd never get around.
*Chorus*

5. Will you wear beige, etc.
No, I won't wear beige,
For it shows my age.
*Chorus*

6. Will you wear black, etc.
No, I won't wear black.
It's the color of a sack.
*Chorus*

7. What will you wear?, etc.
Oh, what do you care
If I just go bare?
*Chorus*

# MISTER RABBIT

**CHORDS USED IN THIS SONG:**

D        A7   or   A7

**CAPO III: Key of F**

**SUGGESTED STRUM:**

Southern

A7

Count: 1    2

Thumb Pluck: thumb plucks the root (R) of the chord; fingers pluck the treble strings on 2.

First Note

Moderate

D

"Mis-ter Rab-bit, Mis-ter Rab-bit, Your ears might-y long!"

"Yes in-deed, they're put on wrong."—

Chorus

A7    D

Ev-'ry lit-tle soul must shine, shine, shine.—

A7    D

Ev-'ry lit-tle soul must shine,— shine, shine.

2. Mister Rabbit, Mister Rabbit,
   Your foot's mighty red!
   "Yes, indeed, I'm almost dead." *(etc.)*

3. Mister Rabbit, Mister Rabbit,
   Your coat's mighty gray!
   "Yes, indeed, 'twas made that way." *(etc.)*

4. Mister Rabbit, Mister Rabbit,
   Your tail's mighty white!
   "Yes, indeed, I'm getting out of sight." *(etc.)*

5. Mister Rabbit, Mister Rabbit,
   You hop mighty high!
   "Yes, indeed, up to the sky." *(etc.)*

64

# I'VE BEEN WORKING ON THE RAILROAD

**CHORDS USED IN THIS SONG:**

**SUGGESTED STRUM:**

Folk Song

G or G   C or C

A7 or A7   B7 or B7   D7

First Note

Moderato

*Count:* 1   2   3   4

Brush strum: index and middle fingers strum downward across the strings.

I've been work-ing on the rail - road, All the live long day;

I've been work-ing on the rail - road just to pass the time a - way.

Don't you hear the whis - tle blow - ing, Rise up so ear - ly in the morn:

Don't you hear the cap - tain shout - ing: "Di - nah, blow your horn!"

**A little faster**

Di-nah won't you blow, Di-nah won't you blow, Di - nah won't you blow your horn;____
Di-nah won't you blow, Di-nah won't you blow, Di - nah won't you blow your

horn. Some-one's in the kitch-en with Di - nah, Some-one's in the kitch-en I know,____

Some-one's in the kitch-en with Di - nah, Strum-min' on the old ban - jo.

Fee, Fie, Fid-dle - ee - I - O, Fee, Fie, Fid-dle - ee - I - O, _____

Fee, Fie, Fid - dle - ee - I - O, Strum-min' on the old ban - jo.

# MICHAEL FINNEGAN

**Traditional**

**CHORDS USED IN THIS SONG:**

**SUGGESTED STRUM:**

G or G    D7

A7

Count: 1    2

Thumb Brush strum: thumb plucks the root (R)
of the chord; fingers brush downward.

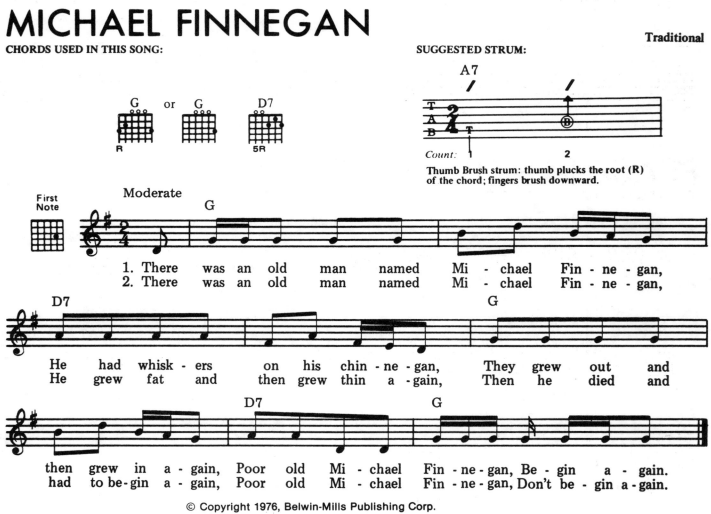

Moderate

G

1. There was an old man named Mi - chael Fin - ne - gan,
2. There was an old man named Mi - chael Fin - ne - gan,

D7    G

He had whisk - ers on his chin - ne - gan, They grew out and
He grew fat and then grew thin a - gain, Then he died and

D7    G

then grew in a - gain, Poor old Mi - chael Fin - ne - gan, Be - gin a - gain.
had to be - gin a - gain, Poor old Mi - chael Fin - ne - gan, Don't be - gin a - gain.

# TEN LITTLE INDIANS

Traditional

**CHORDS USED IN THIS SONG:**

D   A7  or  A7
5R   R5

**SUGGESTED STRUM:**

A7

Count: 1   2 an 3 an 4

Thumb Scratch variation: thumb plucks the root (R) of the chord; optional — thumb plucks the fifth (5) of the chord on 3.

**CAPO III: Key of F**

First Note

Moderate

D

One lit - tle, two lit - tle, three lit - tle In - dians, Four lit -tle, five lit - tle,
Sev'n lit - tle, eight lit - tle, nine lit - tle In - dians,

1.
A7

2.
A7                                          D

six lit - tle In - dians,   Ten lit - tle In - dian boys.

© Copyright 1976, Belwin-Mills Publishing Corp., Melville, N.Y.

# PEASE PORRIDGE HOT

Traditional

**CHORDS USED IN THIS SONG:**

D   G  or  G   A7  or  A7

**SUGGESTED STRUM:**

A7

Count: 1   2 an 3   4

Brush/Scratch variation: give emphasis to the first beat of the measure.

First Note

Brightly

D           G       D    A7     D    A7    D

Pease por - ridge hot, pease por - ridge cold, Pease por - ridge in the pot, nine days old.

G      D     A7    D      A7    D

Some like it hot,   some like it cold,   Some like it in the pot,   nine days old.

© Copyright 1976, Belwin-Mills Publishing Corp.

# SING YOUR WAY HOME

Camp Song

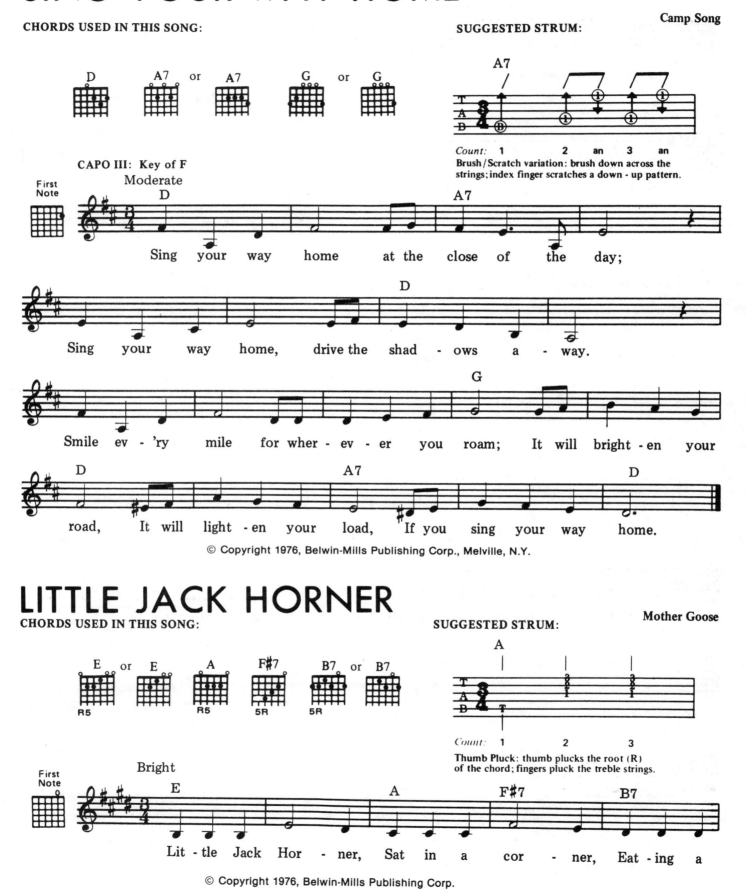

© Copyright 1976, Belwin-Mills Publishing Corp., Melville, N.Y.

# LITTLE JACK HORNER

Mother Goose

© Copyright 1976, Belwin-Mills Publishing Corp.

Christ - mas pie; _____ He put in his thumb and

pulled out a plum, And said, "What a good boy am I!" _____

# THERE WAS A CROOKED MAN

Mother Goose

**CHORDS USED IN THIS SONG:**

**SUGGESTED STRUM:**

There was a crook-ed man, who walked a crook-ed mile, And found a crook-ed six-pence up-on a crook-ed stile, He bought a crook-ed cat that caught a crook-ed mouse and they all lived to-geth-er in a lit-tle crook-ed house.

# THE MORE WE GET TOGETHER

**Traditional**

**CHORDS USED IN THIS SONG:**

**SUGGESTED STRUM:**

*Thumb Brush strum: thumb plucks the root (R) of the chord; fingers brush down across the strings.*

The more we get to - geth - er, to - geth - er, to -

geth - er, The more we get to - geth - er, the hap - p'er we'll

be. For your friends are my friends and my friends are

your friends. The more we get to - geth - er, the hap - pier we'll be.

# IF YOU'RE HAPPY

**CHORDS USED IN THIS SONG:**

**Traditional**

**SUGGESTED STRUM:**

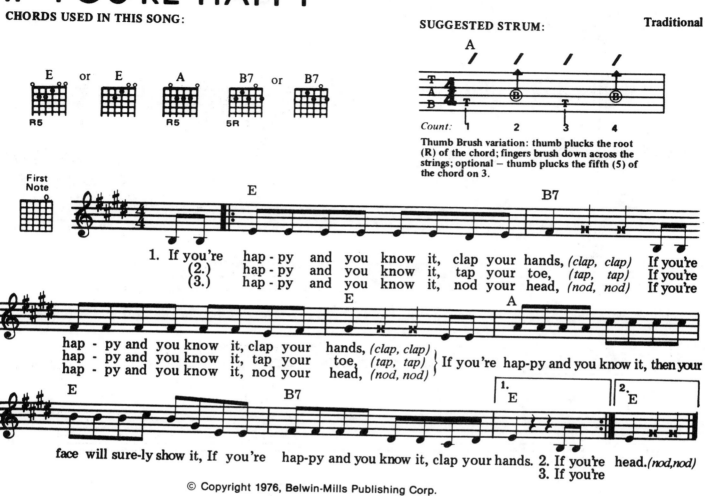

Count:  1  2  3  4

Thumb Brush variation: thumb plucks the root (R) of the chord; fingers brush down across the strings; optional — thumb plucks the fifth (5) of the chord on 3.

**E** or **E**  **A**  **B7** or **B7**

First Note

**E**

**B7**

1. If you're hap - py and you know it, clap your hands, *(clap, clap)* If you're
(2.) hap - py and you know it, tap your toe, *(tap, tap)* If you're
(3.) hap - py and you know it, nod your head, *(nod, nod)* If you're

**E**  **A**

hap - py and you know it, clap your hands, *(clap, clap)*
hap - py and you know it, tap your toe, *(tap, tap)* } If you're hap-py and you know it, then your
hap - py and you know it, nod your head, *(nod, nod)*

**E**  **B7**  1. **E**  2. **E**

face will sure-ly show it, If you're hap-py and you know it, clap your hands. 2. If you're  head. *(nod, nod)*
3. If you're

© Copyright 1976, Belwin-Mills Publishing Corp.

# THE OLD BRASS WAGON

Southern

**CHORDS USED IN THIS SONG:**

G or G    D7    C or C

**SUGGESTED STRUM:**

*Count:* **1** an **2** an **3** an **4** an
Thumb/Finger strum: sweep downward across the
strings; scratch an up - down pattern.

Cir - cle to the left, the old brass wa - gon, Cir - cle to the left, the

old brass wa - gon, Cir-cle to the left, the old brass wa - gon, You're the one, my dar - ling.

**Chorus**

Swing oh swing the old brass wa - gon, Swing oh swing the old brass wa - gon,

Swing oh swing the old brass wa - gon, You're the one my dar - ling.

2. Circle to the right, etc.

3. Swing your gal around, etc.

4. Bring the wagon in, the old brass wagon,
   Take the wagon out, the old brass wagon, etc.

© Copyright 1976, Belwin-Mills Publishing Corp.

# LADYBIRD, LADYBIRD

**CHORDS USED IN THIS SONG:**

Mother Goose

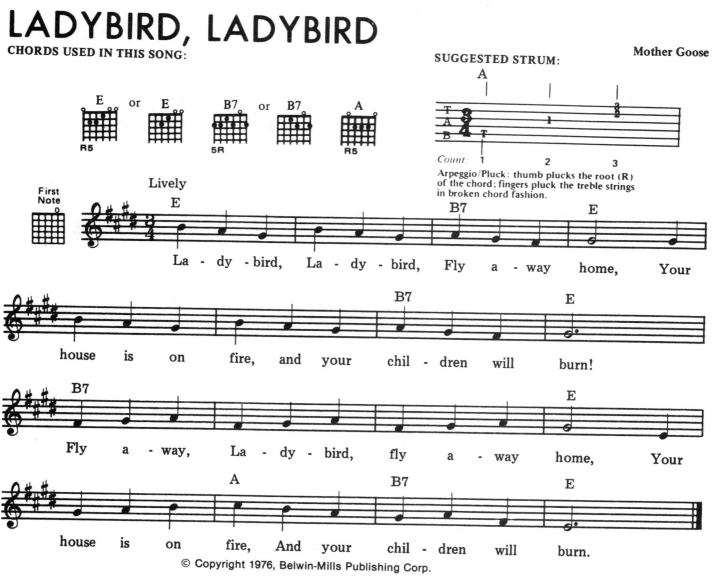

La - dy - bird, La - dy - bird, Fly a - way home, Your

house is on fire, and your chil - dren will burn!

Fly a - way, La - dy - bird, fly a - way home, Your

house is on fire, And your chil - dren will burn.

# OVER THE RIVER

Traditional

**CHORDS USED IN THIS SONG:**

D  G  G  E7  E7  A7

**SUGGESTED STRUM:**

Count: 1 - an  ah  2 - an  ah
Plucking arpeggio: give emphasis to 1 and 2.

First Note

Brightly

1. O - ver the ri - ver and through the wood, To grand-fa-ther's house we
2. O - ver the ri - ver and through the wood, And straight through the barn - yard

go; _____ The horse knows the way to car - ry the sleigh through the
gate, _____ We seem to go ex - treme - ly slow, It

white and drift - ed snow. _____ O - ver the ri - ver and
is so hard to wait! _____ O - ver the ri - ver and

through the wood, Oh how the wind does blow! _____ It
through the wood, Now grand-moth-er's cap I spy! _____ Hur -

stings the toes and bites the nose as o - ver the ground we go! _____
rah for the fun! Is the pud - ding done? Hur - rah for the pump - kin pie! _____

# POP! GOES THE WEASEL

**CHORDS USED IN THIS SONG:**

**SUGGESTED STRUM:**

**Traditional**

D    A7    G or G

**CAPO I: Key of E♭**

Count: 1    2

Brush strum: index and middle fingers strum downward across the strings.

**Moderate**

First Note

D    A7    D    A7

1. A All a-round the cob-bler's bench, the mon-key chased the
2. A pen-ny for a spool__ of thread, a pen-ny for a

D    A7    D    G    A7    D

wea-sel, The mon-key thought t'was all__ in fun. Pop! Goes the wea-sel.
nee-dle, That's the way the mon-ey goes. Pop! Goes the wea-sel.

G    A7    D    G    A7

I've no time to wait__ or sigh, No time to whee-dle,

G    A7    D

On-ly time to say good-bye, Pop! Goes the wea-sel.

© Copyright 1976, Belwin-Mills Publishing Corp.

# A TISKET, A TASKET

**Traditional**

**CHORDS USED IN THIS SONG:**

**SUGGESTED STRUM:**

Thumb Scratch: thumb plucks the root (R) of the chord; optional — thumb plucks the fifth (5) of the chord on 2.

**Moderate**

**C**
A - tis - ket, a tas - ket, a green and yel - low bas - ket, I

**G7** ... **C**
wrote a let - ter to my love and on the way I dropped it, I

dropped it, I dropped it, and on the way I dropped it, A

**G7** ... **C**
lit - tle boy picked it up and put it in his poc - ket.
(girl) (her)

© Copyright 1976, Belwin-Mills Publishing Corp.

# EENCY WEENCY SPIDER

**Traditional**

CHORDS USED IN THIS SONG:

E or E     B7 or B7

R5          5R

SUGGESTED STRUM:

E

Count: 1   2

Brush strum: index and middle fingers strum downward across the strings.

First Note

Moderate

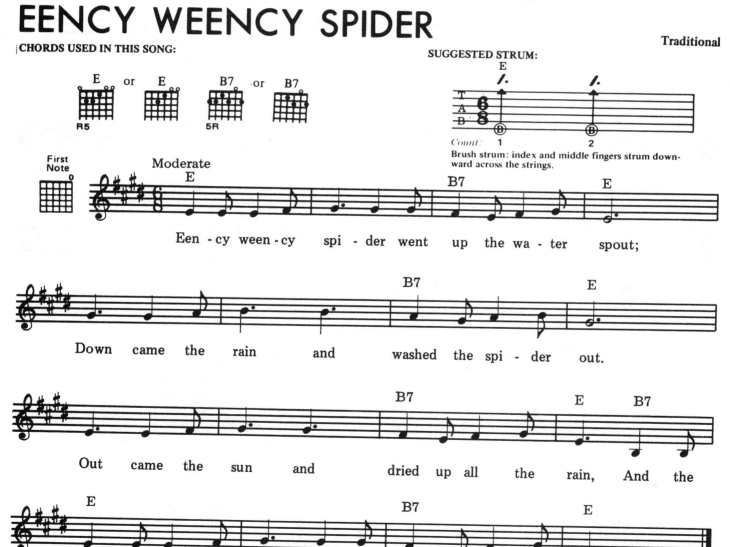

Een - cy ween - cy spi - der went up the wa - ter spout;

Down came the rain and washed the spi - der out.

Out came the sun and dried up all the rain, And the

een - cy ween - cy spi - der went up the spout a - gain.

# IT'S RAINING

German Folk Song

**CHORDS USED IN THIS SONG:**

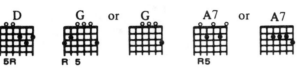

**SUGGESTED STRUM:**

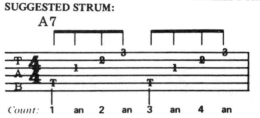

Count: 1 an 2 an 3 an 4 an

Arpeggio variation: thumb plucks the root (R) of the chord; fingers pluck the treble strings; optional — thumb plucks the fifth (5) of the chord on 3.

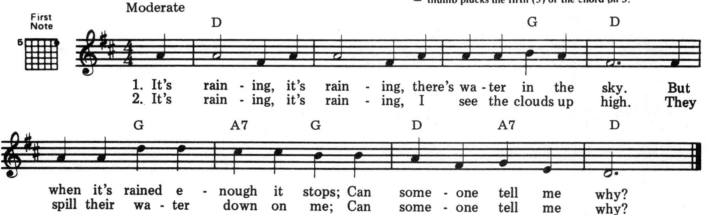

1. It's rain - ing, it's rain - ing, there's wa - ter in the sky. But
2. It's rain - ing, it's rain - ing, I see the clouds up high. They

when it's rained e - nough it stops; Can some - one tell me why?
spill their wa - ter down on me; Can some - one tell me why?

© Copyright 1976, Belwin-Mills Publishing Corp., Melville, N.Y.

# JOHN JACOB JINGLEHEIMER SCHMIDT

Traditional

**CHORDS USED IN THIS SONG:**

**SUGGESTED STRUM:**

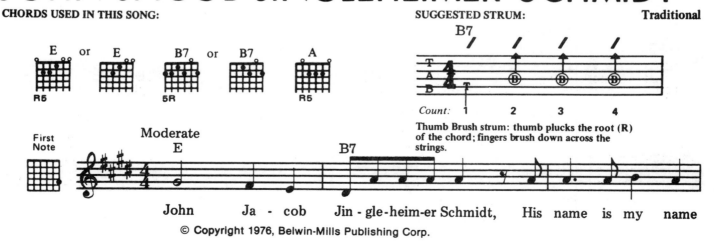

Count: 1 2 3 4

Thumb Brush strum: thumb plucks the root (R) of the chord; fingers brush down across the strings.

John Ja - cob Jin - gle-heim-er Schmidt, His name is my name

© Copyright 1976, BELWIN-MILLS Publishing Corp.

too! When - ev - er I go out, The peo - ple al - ways shout,

"John Ja - cob Jin - gle - heim - er Schmidt, "Dah dah dah dah dah dah dah dah.

# TWINKLE, TWINKLE, LITTLE STAR

**CHORDS USED IN THIS SONG:**

**SUGGESTED STRUM:**

**Traditional**

D   G or G   A7 or A7

A7

Count: 1   2   3   4

Brush strum: index and middle fingers strum
downward across the strings.

First Note

Moderately

D          G   D   G   D   A7   D   *Fine*

1. Twin - kle, twin - kle, lit - tle star, How I won - der what you are
2. Twin - kle, twin - kle, lit - tle star, How I won - der what you are

*D. C. al Fine*

Up a - bove the world so high. Like a dia - mond in the sky.

# SOME FOLKS DO

**Traditional**

**CHORDS USED IN THIS SONG:**

E or E    B7 or B7    A

**SUGGESTED STRUM:**

B7

*Count:* **1** an **2** an **3** an **4** an
Thumb/Finger strum: sweep downward across the
strings; scratch an up - down pattern.

First Note

Moderate

1. Some folks like to sigh, Some folks do, some folks do,
2. Some folks got grey hair, Some folks do, some folks do,

Some folks long to die, But that's not me nor you.
Brood - ing o - ver cares, But that's not me nor you.

Long live the mer-ry mer-ry heart that laughs by night and day, Like the

Queen of Mirth, No mat - ter what some folks say.

© Copyright 1976, Belwin-Mills Publishing Corp.

# HERE WE GO ROUND THE MULBERRY BUSH

Mother Goose

**CHORDS USED IN THIS SONG:**

E or E    B7 or B7

**SUGGESTED STRUM:**

*Count:* 1   an   ah   2   an   ah

Thumb pluck pattern: thumb plucks the root (R) of the chord.

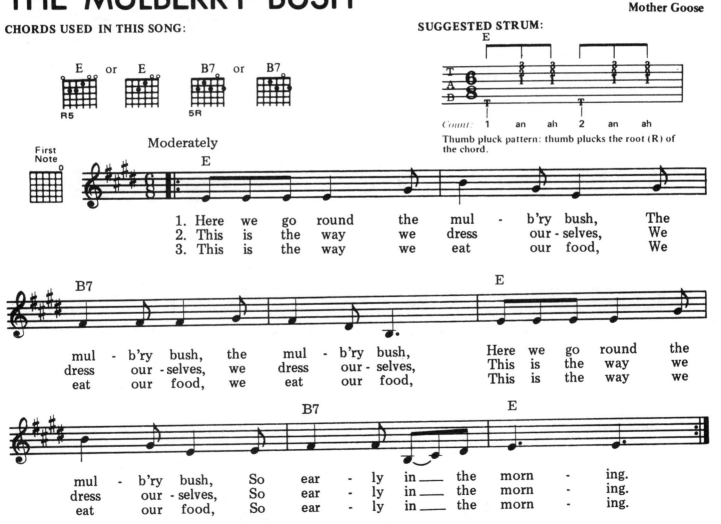

First Note

Moderately

E

1. Here we go round the mul - b'ry bush, The
2. This is the way we dress our - selves, We
3. This is the way we eat our food, We

B7                                                    E

mul - b'ry bush, the mul - b'ry bush,      Here we go round the
dress our - selves, we dress our - selves,   This is the way we
eat our food, we eat our food,              This is the way we

B7                          E

mul - b'ry bush, So ear - ly in the morn - ing.
dress our - selves, So ear - ly in the morn - ing.
eat our food, So ear - ly in the morn - ing.

# THIS OLD MAN

**Traditional**

**CHORDS USED IN THIS SONG:**

D    A7

5R    R5

**SUGGESTED STRUM:**

Count: 1    an    2    an

Thumb Scratch: thumb plucks the root (**R**) of the chord; optional — thumb plucks the fifth (5) of the chord on 2.

Moderate

First Note
5

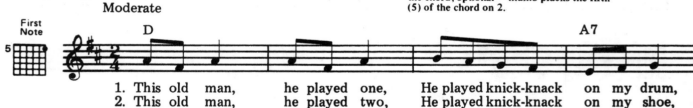

1. This old man,    he played one,    He played knick-knack    on my drum,
2. This old man,    he played two,    He played knick-knack    on my shoe,

Chorus

Knick-knack, pad-dy whack, give the dog a bone,    This old man came    roll - ing home.

3. This old man, he played three
   He played knick-knack on my knee. (Chorus)

4. This old man, he played four,
   He played knick-knack on my door. (Chorus)

5. This old man, he played five,
   He played knick-knack on my hive. (Chorus)

6. This old man, he played six,
   He played knick-knack on my sticks. (Chorus)

7. This old man, he played seven,
   He played knick-knack up to heaven. (Chorus)

8. This old man, he played eight,
   He played knick-knack at the gate. (Chorus)

9. This old man, he played nine,
   He played knick-knack on my line. (Chorus)

10. This old man, he played ten,
    He played knick-knack over again. (Chorus)

# SHOO, FLY

Traditional

**CHORDS USED IN THIS SONG:**

**SUGGESTED STRUM:**

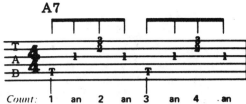

Count: 1 an 2 an 3 an 4 an

Plucking/Arpeggio pattern: thumb plucks the root (R) of the chord; fingers pluck the treble strings: optional — alternate to the fifth (5) of the chord on 3.

**CAPO III: Key of F**

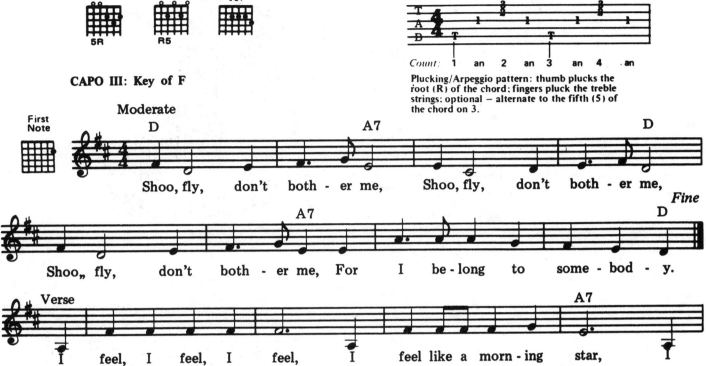

Moderate

D       A7       D

Shoo, fly, don't both - er me, Shoo, fly, don't both - er me,

A7       D    *Fine*

Shoo, fly, don't both - er me, For I be - long to some - bod - y.

Verse       A7

I feel, I feel, I feel, I feel like a morn - ing star,

D    *D. C. al Fine*

feel, I feel, I feel, I feel like a morn - ing star.

© Copyright 1976, Belwin-Mills Publishing Corp.

# OLD MacDONALD HAD A FARM

**Traditional**

**CHORDS USED IN THIS SONG:**

**SUGGESTED STRUM:**

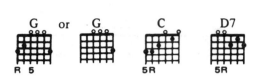

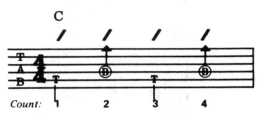

*Count:* 1    2    3    4

**Thumb Brush variation:** thumb plucks the root (R) of the chord; fingers brush down across the strings; optional — thumb plucks the fifth (5) of the chord on 3.

1. Old Mac - Don - ald had a farm, E - I - E - I -

O! And on this farm he had a duck, E - I - E - I -

O! With a quack-quack here, and a quack-quack there, Here a quack, there a quack,

Ev-'ry - where a quack, quack. Old Mac-Don - ald had a farm, E - I - E - I - O!

2. Old MacDonald had a farm,
   E - I - E - I - O!
   And on this farm he had a chick,
   E - I - E - I - O!
   With a chick, chick here
   And a chick, chick there,
   Here a chick, there a chick,
   Everywhere a chick, chick
   Old MacDonald had a farm,
   E - I - E - I - O!

Other verses

3. Cow — moo, moo
4. Dogs — bow, wow
5. Pigs — oink, oink
6. Rooster — cock-a-doodle, dock-a-doodle
7. Turkey — gobble, gobble
8. Cat — meow, meow
9. Horse — neigh, neigh
10. Donkey — hee-haw, hee-haw

# THE FARMER IN THE DELL

Traditional

**CHORDS USED IN THIS SONG:**

**SUGGESTED STRUM:**

D  A7

**CAPO III: Key of F**

Count:  1  2

Thumb Brush strum: thumb plucks the root (R) of the chord; fingers brush downward.

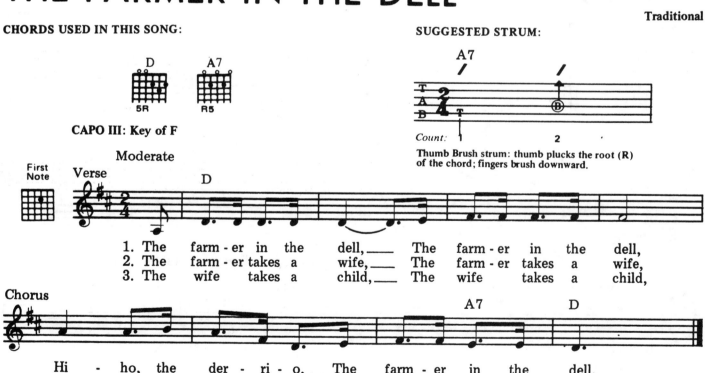

First Note

Moderate

**Verse**

D

1. The farm-er in the dell,___ The farm-er in the dell,
2. The farm-er takes a wife,___ The farm-er takes a wife,
3. The wife takes a child,___ The wife takes a child,

**Chorus**

A7  D

Hi - ho, the der - ri - o, The farm-er in the dell.

4. The child takes a nurse, etc.

5. The nurse takes a dog, etc.

6. The dog takes a cat, etc.

7. The cat takes the rat, etc.

8. The rat takes the cheese, etc.

9. The cheese stands alone, etc.

# BINGO

**Traditional**

**CHORDS USED IN THIS SONG:**

**SUGGESTED STRUM:**

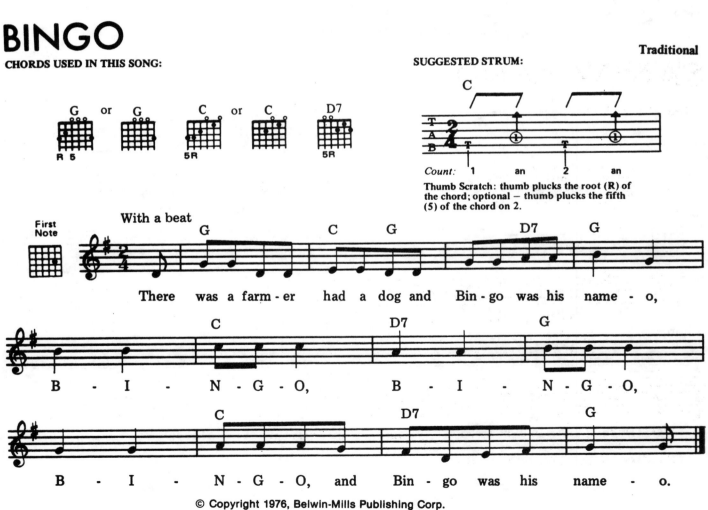

*Thumb Scratch:* thumb plucks the root (R) of the chord; optional — thumb plucks the fifth (5) of the chord on 2.

**With a beat**

There was a farm-er had a dog and Bin-go was his name - o,

B - I - N - G - O, B - I - N - G - O,

B - I - N - G - O, and Bin-go was his name - o.

# HEY, HO, NOBODY HOME

Traditional

CHORDS USED IN THIS SONG:

SUGGESTED STRUM:

Sweep/Brush strum: thumb sweeps downward; fingers strum downward.

Hey, ho, no - bod - y home? Meat and drink and mon - ey have I none; Yet I will be mer - ry. ___

# SANDY LAND

Traditional

CHORDS USED IN THIS SONG:

SUGGESTED STRUM:

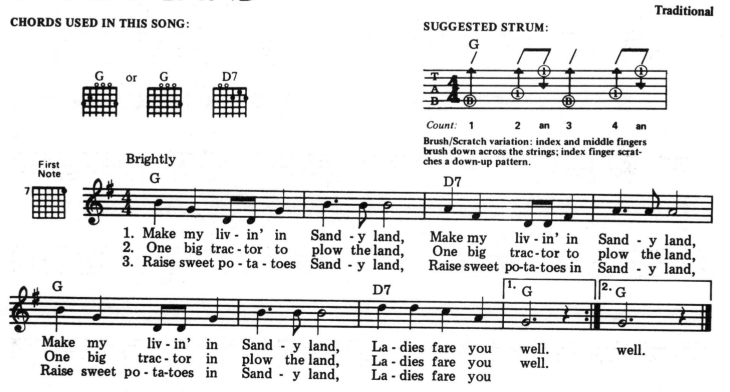

Brush/Scratch variation: index and middle fingers brush down across the strings; index finger scratches a down-up pattern.

1. Make my liv - in' in Sand - y land, Make my liv - in' in Sand - y land,
2. One big trac - tor to plow the land, One big trac - tor to plow the land,
3. Raise sweet po - ta - toes Sand - y land, Raise sweet po - ta - toes in Sand - y land,

Make my liv - in' in Sand - y land, La - dies fare you well. well.
One big trac - tor in plow the land, La - dies fare you well.
Raise sweet po - ta - toes in Sand - y land, La - dies fare you

# SHE'LL BE COMIN' 'ROUND THE MOUNTAIN

**Traditional**

**CHORDS USED IN THIS SONG:**

**SUGGESTED STRUM:**

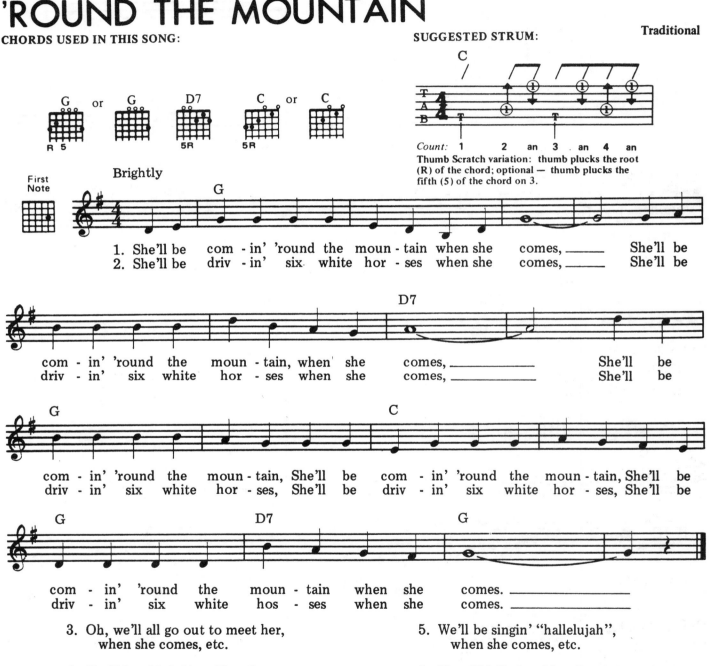

1. She'll be comin' 'round the mountain when she comes, _____ She'll be
2. She'll be drivin' six white horses when she comes, _____ She'll be

comin' 'round the mountain, when she comes, _____ She'll be
drivin' six white horses when she comes, _____ She'll be

comin' 'round the moun-tain, She'll be comin' 'round the moun-tain, She'll be
drivin' six white hor-ses, She'll be drivin' six white hor-ses, She'll be

comin' 'round the moun-tain when she comes. _____
drivin' six white hos-ses when she comes. _____

3. Oh, we'll all go out to meet her,
   when she comes, etc.

4. She'll be shinin' just like silver,
   when she comes, etc.

5. She'll be breathin' smoke and fire,
   when she comes, etc.

5. We'll be singin' "hallelujah",
   when she comes, etc.

6. We will kill the old red rooster,
   when she comes, etc.

7. And we'll all have chick'n and dumplin's,
   when she comes, etc.

# SKIP TO MY LOU

**Traditional**

**CHORDS USED IN THIS SONG:**

**SUGGESTED STRUM:**

*Count:* 1 an 2 an

Thumb Scratch: thumb plucks the root (R) of the chord; optional — thumb plucks the fifth (5) of the chord on 2.

First Note

Moderate

1. Skip, skip, skip to the Lou, Skip, skip, skip to the Lou.

Skip, skip, skip to my Lou, Skip to the Lou, my dar - ling.

2. Little red wagon painted blue,
Little red wagon painted blue,
Little red wagon painted blue,
Skip to my Lou, my darling.

3. Flies in the buttermilk, shoo fly shoo,
Flies in the buttermilk, shoo fly shoo,
Flies in the buttermilk, shoo fly shoo,
Skip to my Lou, my darling.

4. Lost my partner, what'll I do,
Lost my partner, what'll I do,
Lost my partner, what'll I do,
Skip to my Lou, my darling.

5. I'll get another one, prettier than you,
I'll get another one, prettier than you,
I'll get another one, prettier than you,
Skip to my Lou, my darling.

# HUSH, LITTLE BABY

**Traditional**

**CHORDS USED IN THIS SONG:**

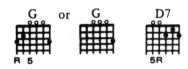

G   or   G        D7

R   5              5R

**SUGGESTED STRUM:**

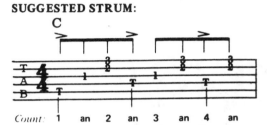

C

Count: 1 an 2 an 3 an 4 an

Rumba pattern: thumb plucks the root (R) of the chord or may alternate to the fifth (5) or 2 an and 4; give emphasis on 1, 2 an and 4.

**Moderate**

1. Hush lit - tle ba - by, don't say a word,
3. If that dia - mond ring turns brass,

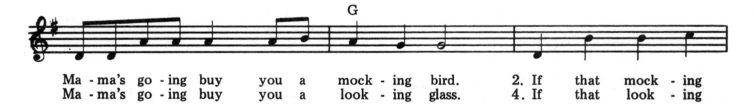

Ma - ma's go - ing buy you a mock - ing bird.   2. If that mock - ing
Ma - ma's go - ing buy you a look - ing glass.   4. If that look - ing

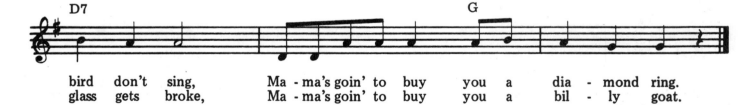

bird don't sing,   Ma - ma's goin' to buy you a dia - mond ring.
glass gets broke,   Ma - ma's goin' to buy you a bil - ly goat.

5. If that billy goat won't pull,
   Mama's goin' to buy you a cart and bull.

6. If that cart and bull turn over,
   Mama's goin' to buy you a dog named Rover.

7. If that dog named Rover won't bark
   Mama's goin' to buy you a horse and cart.

8. If that horse and cart fall down,
   You'll still be the sweetest little baby in town.

# Lullaby

**CHORDS USED IN THIS SONG:**

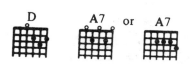

D    A7 or A7

**SUGGESTED STRUM:**

*Count:* 1  2  3  4

Sweep strum: thumb strums downward across the strings.

First Note

**Softly**

1. Hush a - bye, don't you__ cry, Lit - tle stars will see you.
2. Night is__ here, ba - by__ dear, You must go to sleep too.

© Copyright 1976, Belwin-Mills Publishing Corp., Melville, N.Y.

# ARE YOU SLEEPING?

**CHORDS USED IN THIS SONG:**

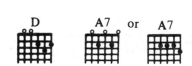

D    A7 or A7

**CAPO III: Key of F**   Note: This song could also be played using the D chord only.

**SUGGESTED STRUM:**

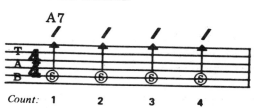

*Count:* 1  2  3  4

Sweep strum: thumb strums downward across the strings.

First Note

**Moderate**

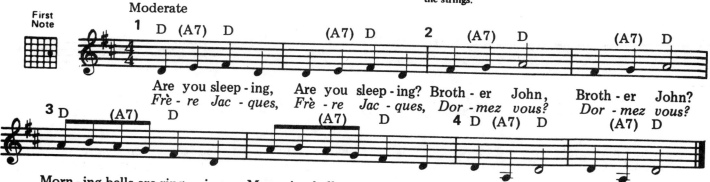

Are you sleep - ing, Are you sleep - ing? Broth - er John, Broth - er John?
Frè - re Jac - ques, Frè - re Jac - ques, Dor - mez vous? Dor - mez vous?

Morn - ing bells are ring - ing, Morn - ing bells are ring - ing, Ding, ding, dong, Ding, ding, dong.
Son - nez les ma - ti - nes, Son - nez les ma - ti - nes, Din, dan, don, Din, dan, don.

© Copyright 1976, Belwin-Mills Publishing Corp.

# LONDON BRIDGE

**CHORDS USED IN THIS SONG:**

Traditional

SUGGESTED STRUM:

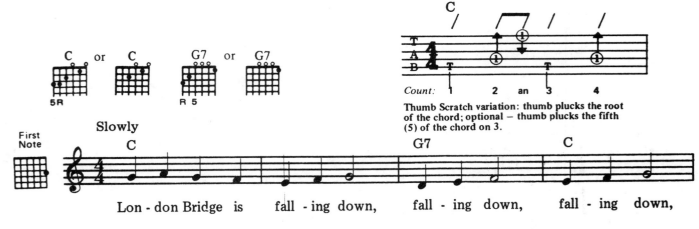

C or C    G7 or G7

Count:  1    2  an  3    4

Thumb Scratch variation: thumb plucks the root
of the chord; optional — thumb plucks the fifth
(5) of the chord on 3.

First Note

Slowly

C                                    G7              C

Lon - don Bridge is    fall - ing down,    fall - ing  down,    fall - ing  down,

G7              C

Lon - don Bridge is    fall - ing down,    My    fair    la - dy.

2. Build it up with sticks and stones,
   Sticks and stones, sticks and stones,
   Build it up with sticks and stones,
   My fair lady.

3. Sticks and stones will bend and break
   Bend and break, bend and break,
   Sticks and stones will bend and break,
   My fair lady.

4. Build it up with iron bars,
   Iron bars, iron bars,
   Build it up with iron bars,
   My fair lady.

5. Iron bars will rust away,
   Rust away, rust away,
   Iron bars will rust away,
   My fair lady.

# ROCK-A-BYE BABY

**Traditional**

**CHORDS USED IN THIS SONG:**

**SUGGESTED STRUM:**

A    E7    or    E7
R5    R5

Arpeggio/Pluck: thumb plucks the root (R) of the chord; fingers pluck the treble strings in broken chord fashion.

Rock - a - bye ba - by on the tree - top,
When the bough breaks by the cra - dle will

When the wind blows the cra - dle will rock,

fall, and down will come ba - by, cra - dle and all.

# THE MUFFIN MAN

**Traditional**

**CHORDS USED IN THIS SONG:**

**SUGGESTED STRUM:**

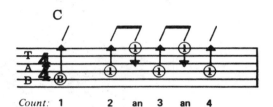

G or G    C or C    D7

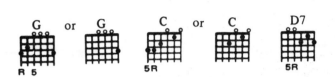

*Count:* 1    2 an 3 an 4

Brush/Scratch variation: brush down with the fingers; scratch a down-up pattern.

**First Note**    **Lively**

G                                    C

D7                G                            D7            G

1. Oh,    do  you  know  the  muf-fin  man,  the  muf-fin  man,  the
2. Oh,    yes  I  know  the  muf-fin  man,  the  muf-fin  man,  the

muf-fin  man.  Oh,  do  you  know  the  muf-fin  man  that  lives  in  Dru-ry  Lane?
muf-fin  man.  Oh,  yes  I  know  the  muf-fin  man  that  lives  in  Dru-ry  Lane.

# RING AROUND THE ROSY

**Traditional**

**CHORDS USED IN THIS SONG:**

**SUGGESTED STRUM:**

C or C    G or G

C

*Count:* 1    an  2    an

Thumb Scratch: thumb plucks the root (R) of the chord; optional — thumb plucks the fifth (5) of the chord on 2.

**First Note**    **Moderate**

C

Ring  a-round  the  ros-y,    Pock-ets  full  of  pos-y,

Ash - es, Ash - es, we all fall down!

# THUMBKIN

**CHORDS USED IN THIS SONG:**

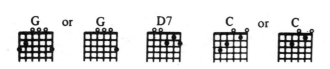

G or G    D7    C or C

**SUGGESTED STRUM:**

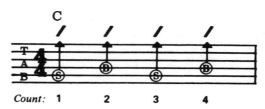

C

*Count:* 1  2  3  4

**Sweep/Brush strum: thumb sweeps downward;
fingers strum downward.**

Not too fast

1. Thumb - kin says, "I'll dance!"  Thumb - kin says, "I'll dance!"
2. Point - er says, "I'll dance!"  Point - er says, "I'll dance!"

Dance and sing ye mer - ry lit - tle men!  Thumb - kin says, "I'll dance!"
Dance and sing ye mer - ry lit - tle men!  Point - er says, "I'll dance!"

3. Tall man says, etc.        5. Little man says, etc.

4. Gold man says, etc.        6. All men say, etc.

© Copyright 1976, Belwin-Mills Publishing Corp.

# COCK ROBIN

**Traditional**

2. Who saw him die? "I", said the fly, "with my little beady eye." (etc.)

3. Who made his shroud-o? "I", said the eagle, "with my little thread and needle." (etc.)

4. Who made his coffin? "I", said the snipe, "with my little pocket knife." (etc.)

5. Who dug his grave-o? "I", said the crow, "with my little pick and hoe." (etc.)

6. Who let him down-o? "I", said the crane, "with my little golden chain." (etc.)

7. Who preached his funeral-o? "I", said the rook, "with my little holy book." (etc.)